Dedicated with love to all those who were
affected by the recent hurricanes and storms
in the US & Caribbean.
May you rebuild and renew
your lives as before.

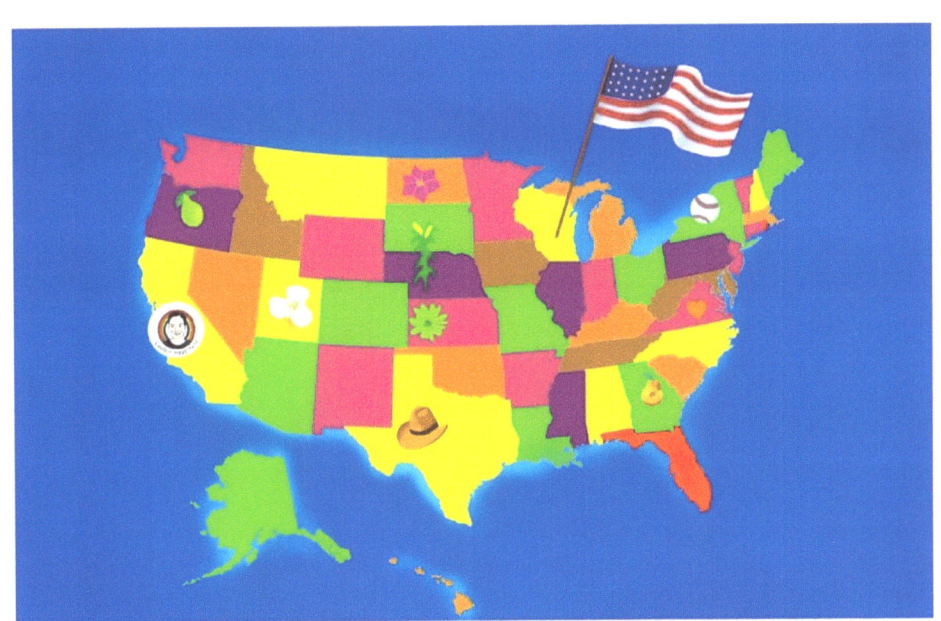

What Life Means to Einstein
An Interview by George Sylvester Viereck

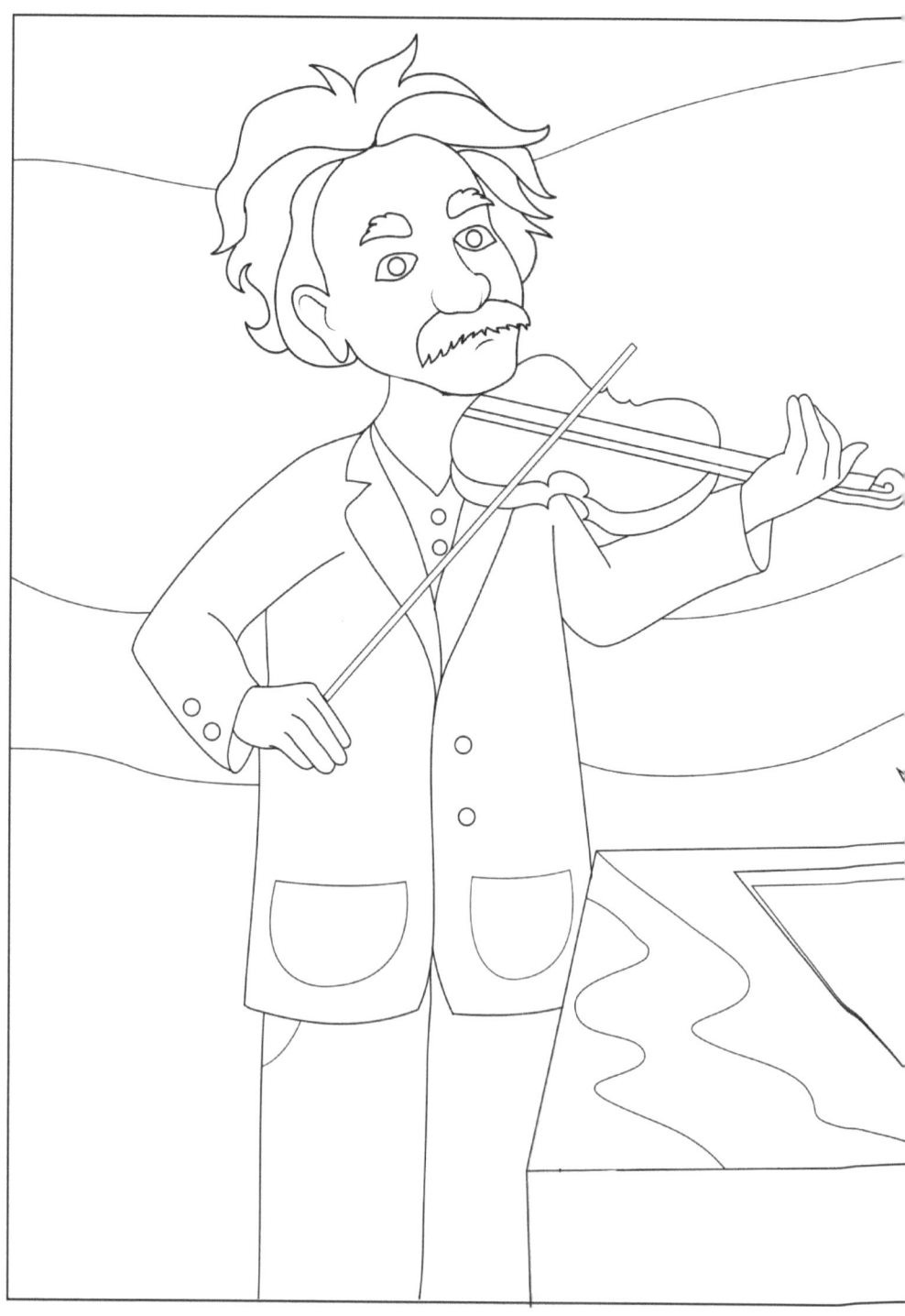

THE SATURDAY EVENING POST - OCTOBER 26, 1929

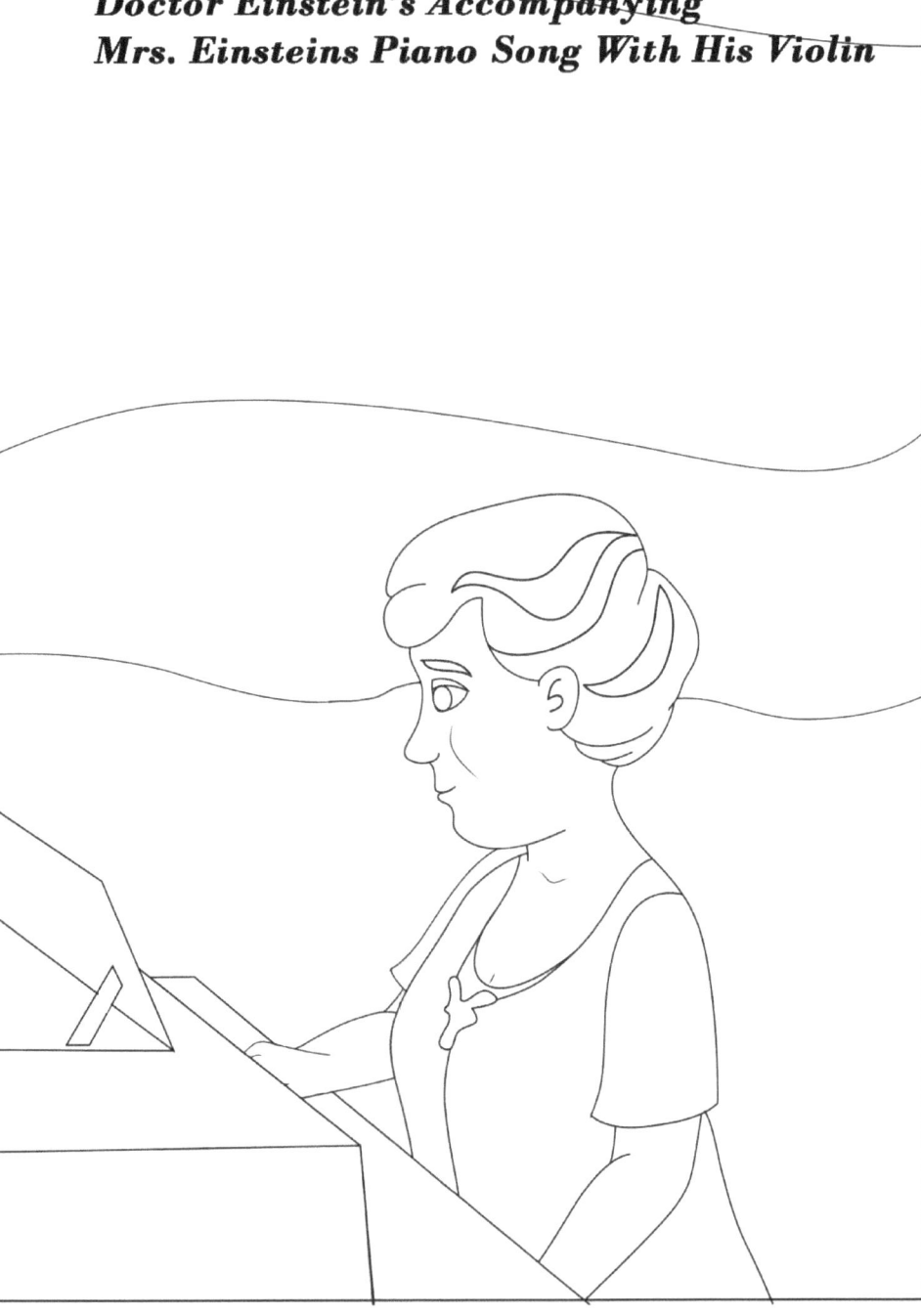

*Doctor Einstein's Accompanying
Mrs. Einsteins Piano Song With His Violin*

What Life Means to Einstein
An Interview by George Sylvester Viereck

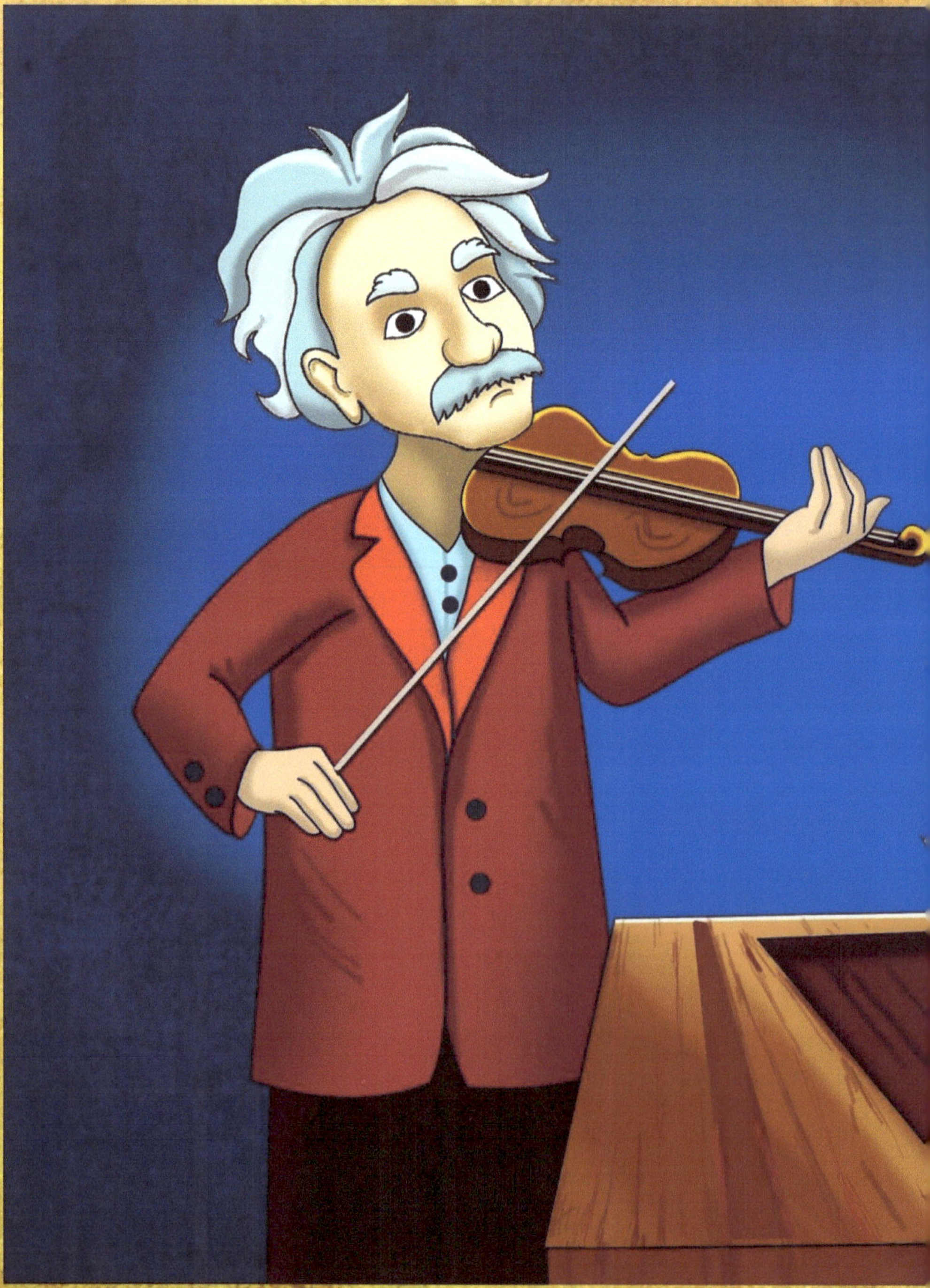

THE SATURDAY EVENING POST - OCTOBER 26, 1929

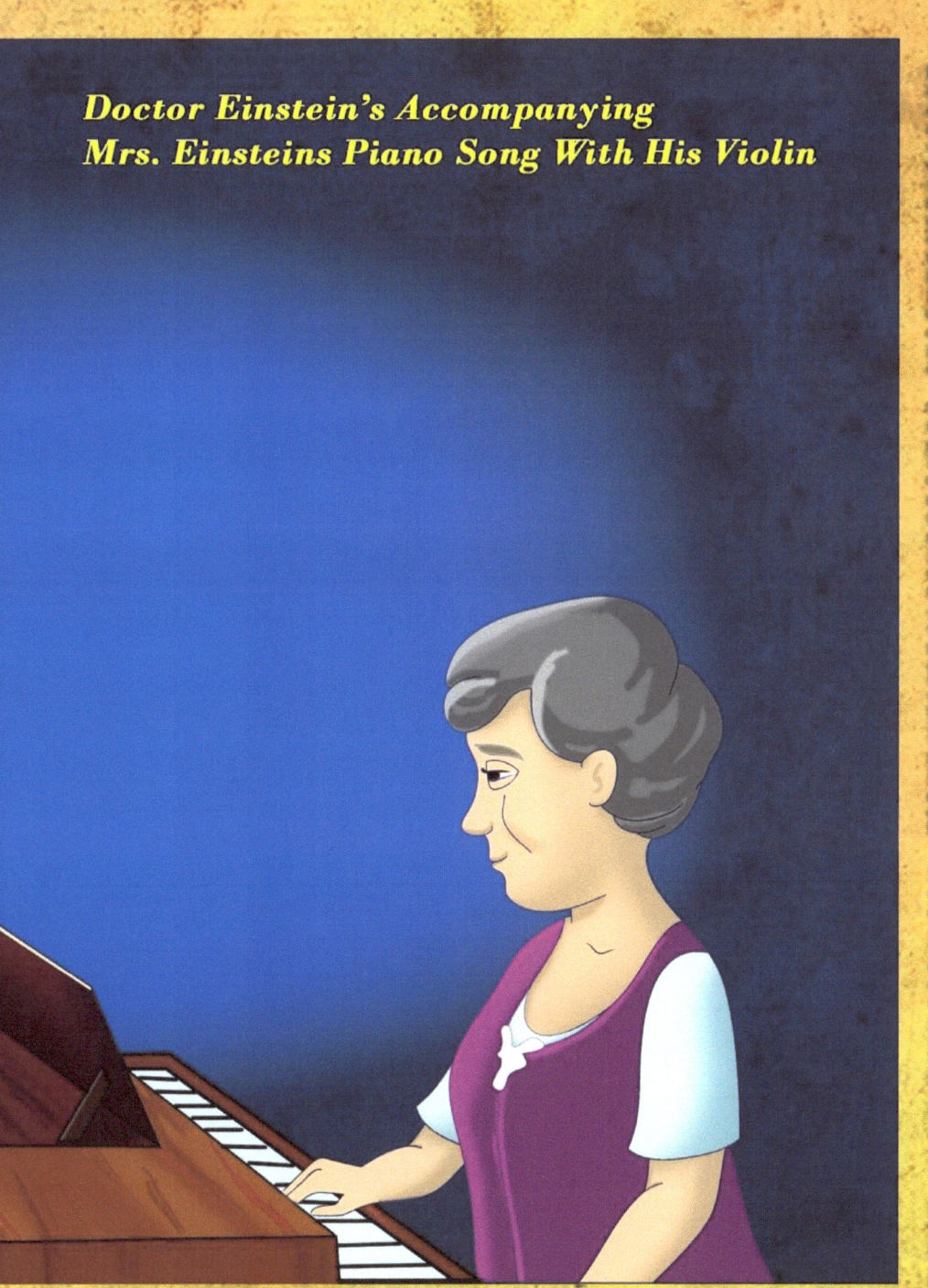

Doctor Einstein's Accompanying Mrs. Einsteins Piano Song With His Violin

Albert Einstein said on October 26, 1929: I am enough of an artist to draw freely upon my imagination.

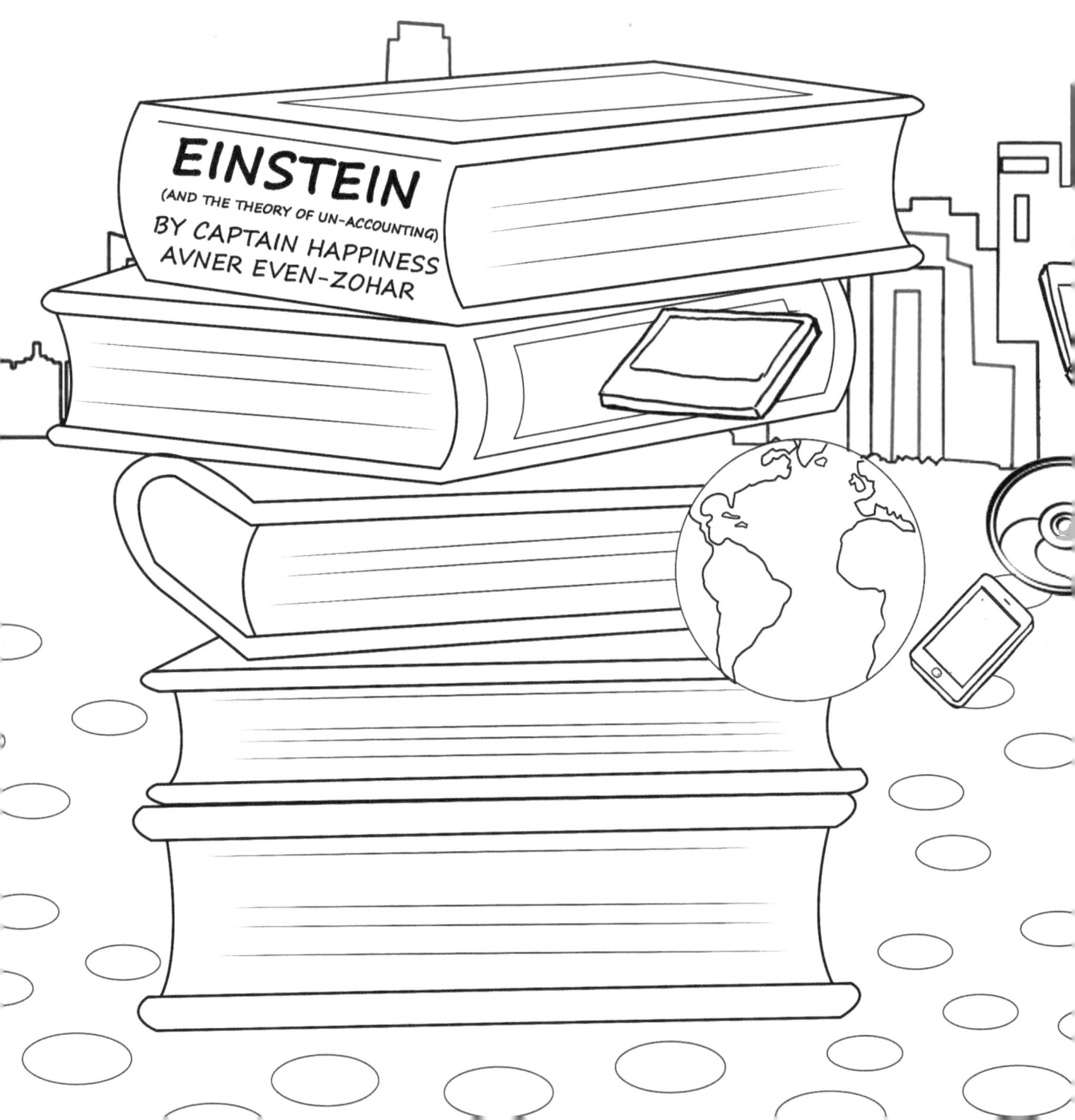

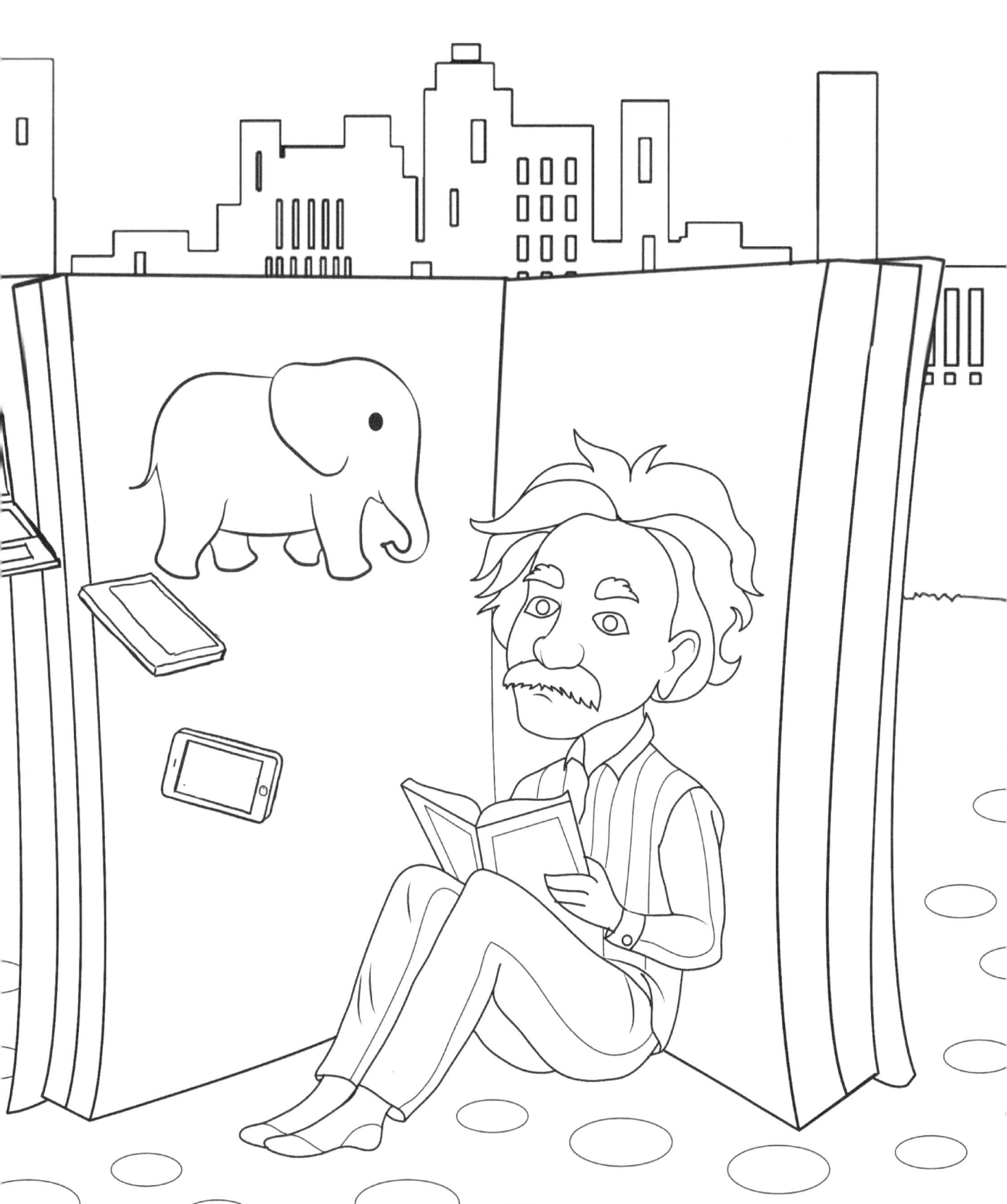

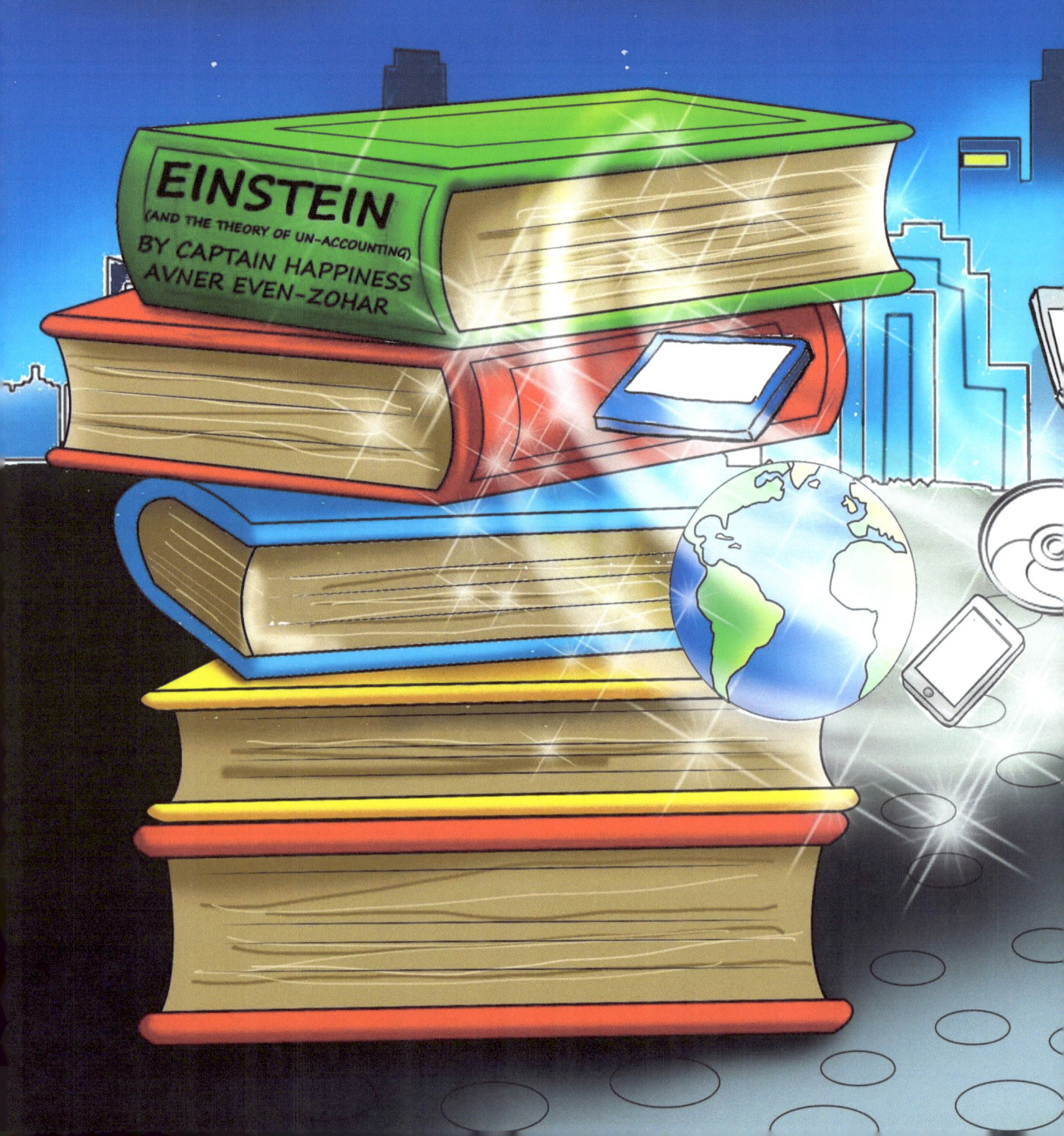

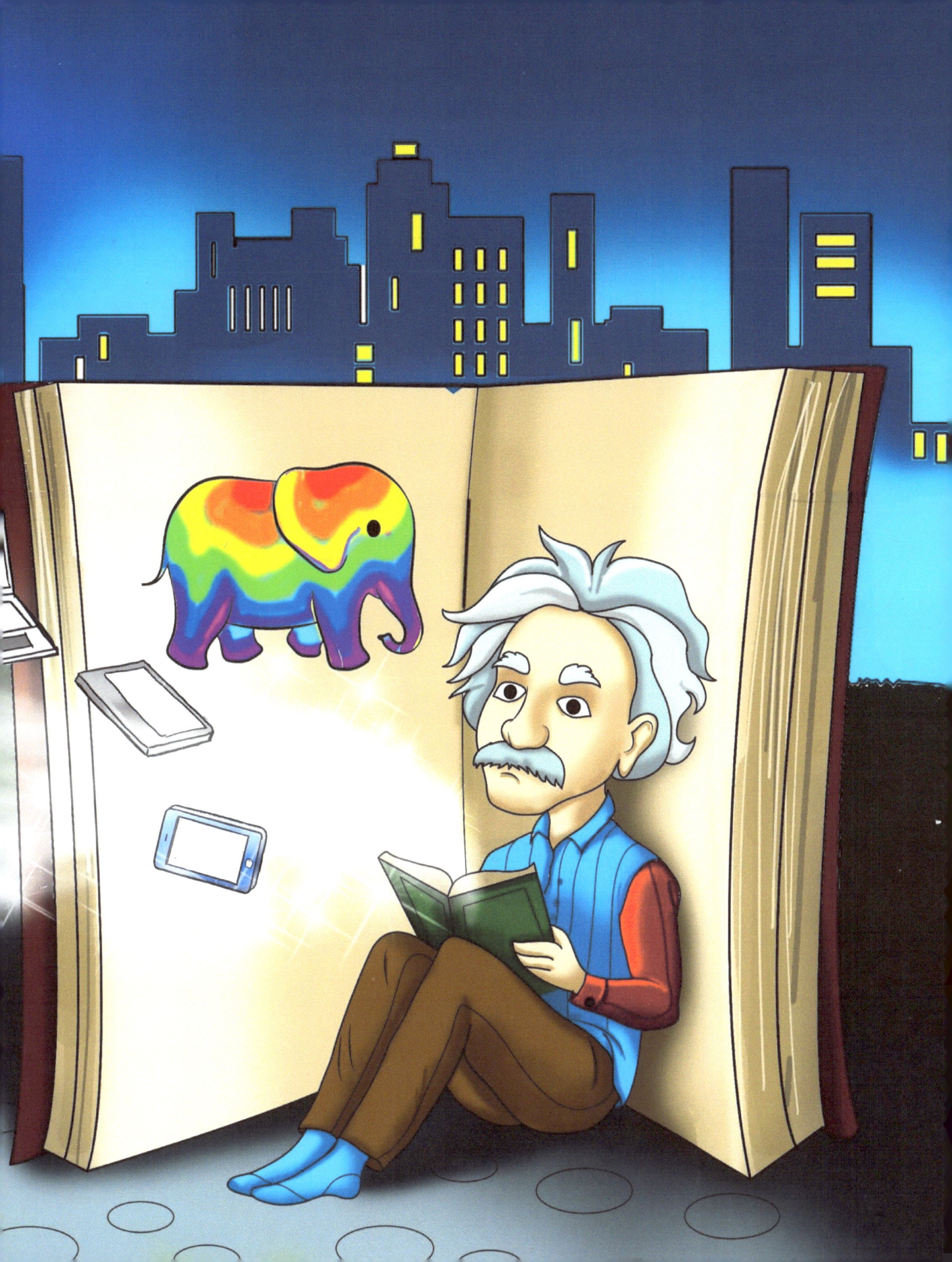

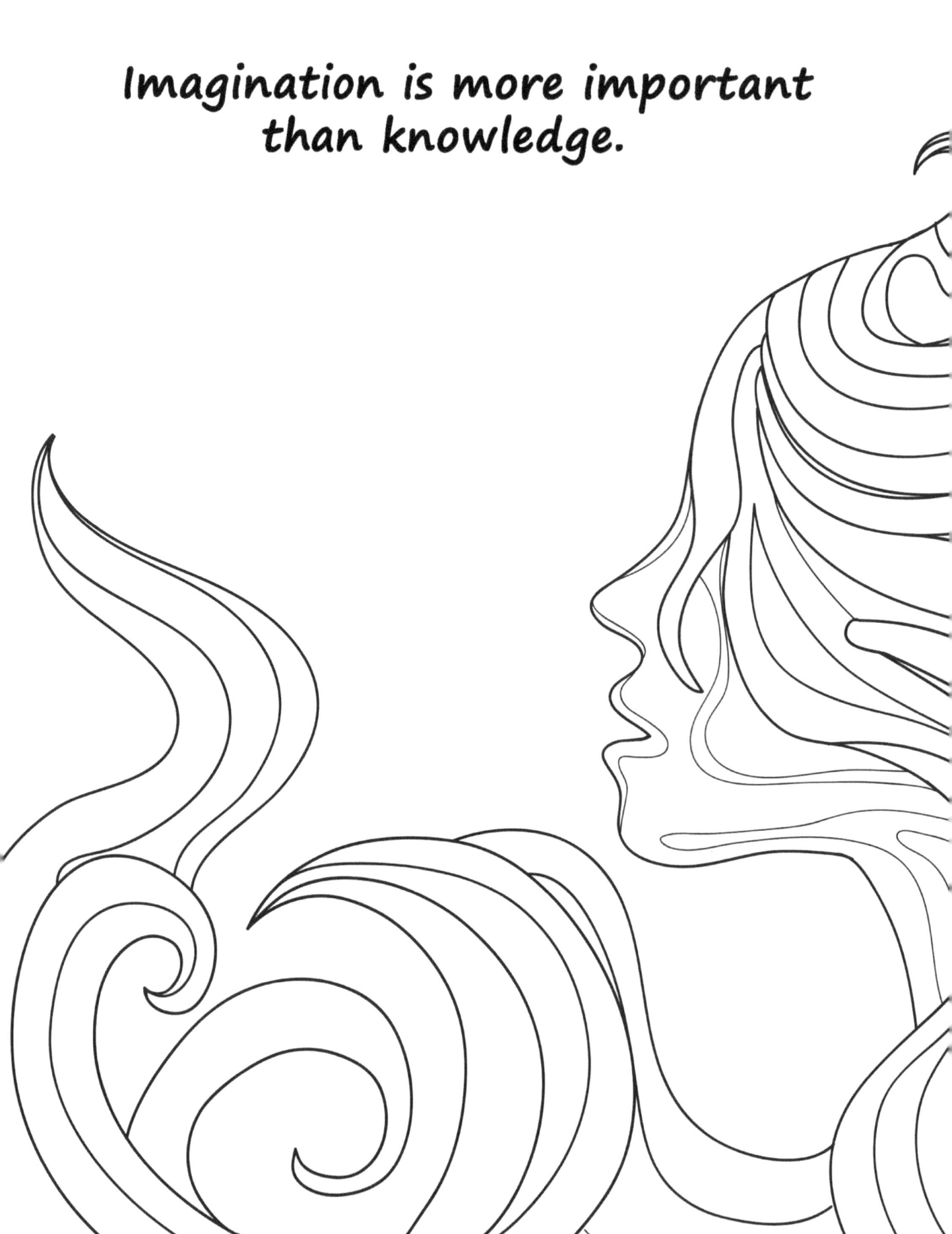

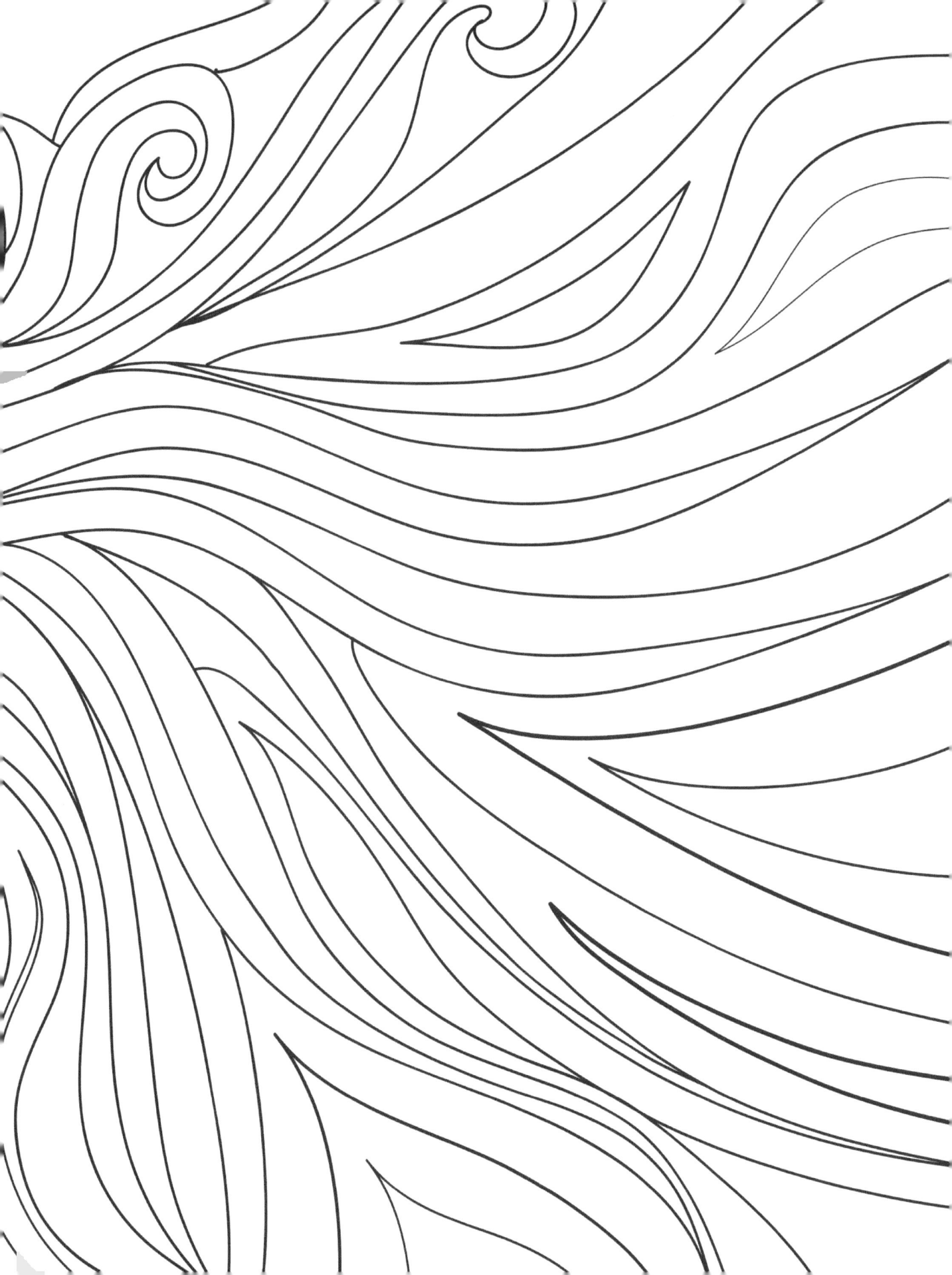

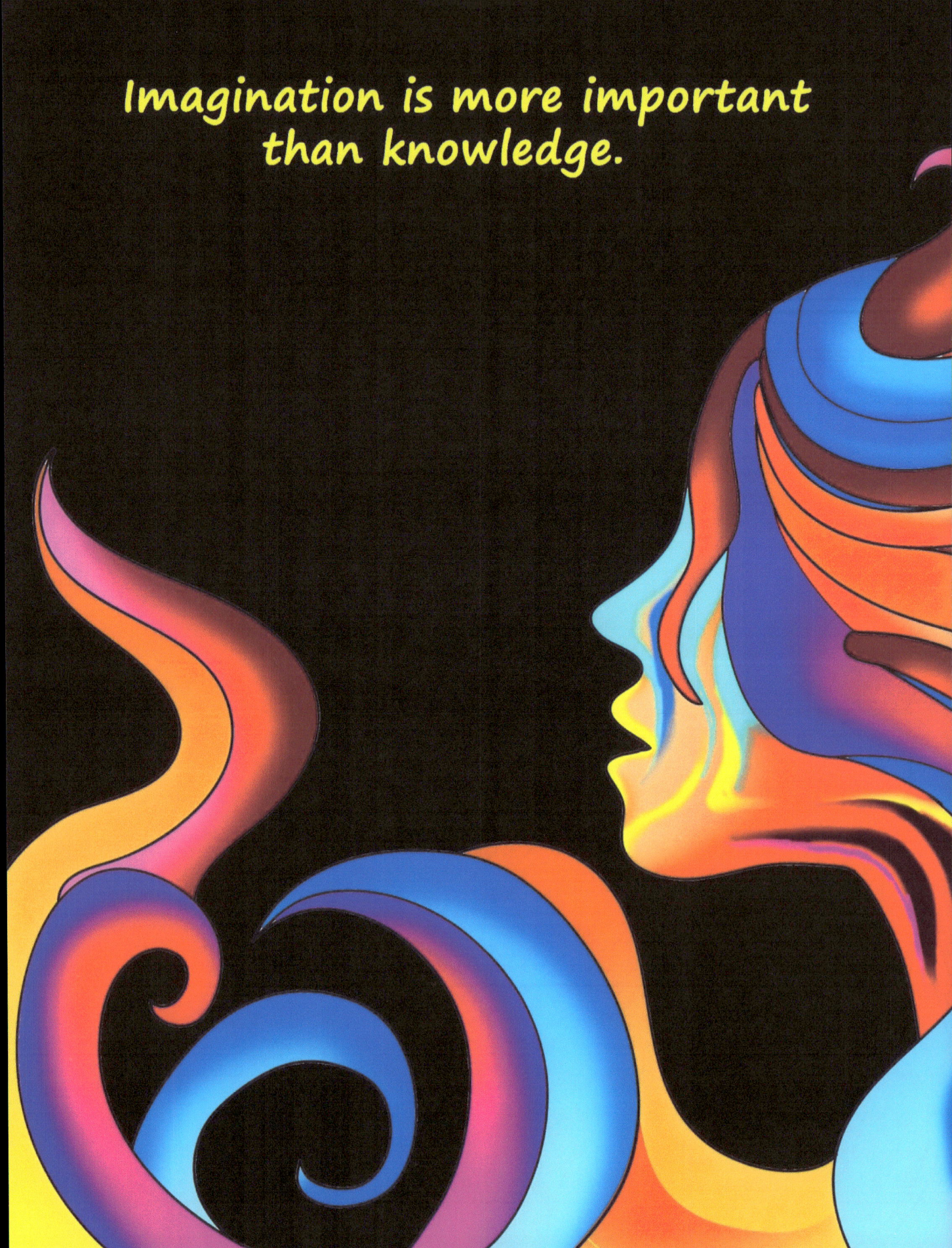

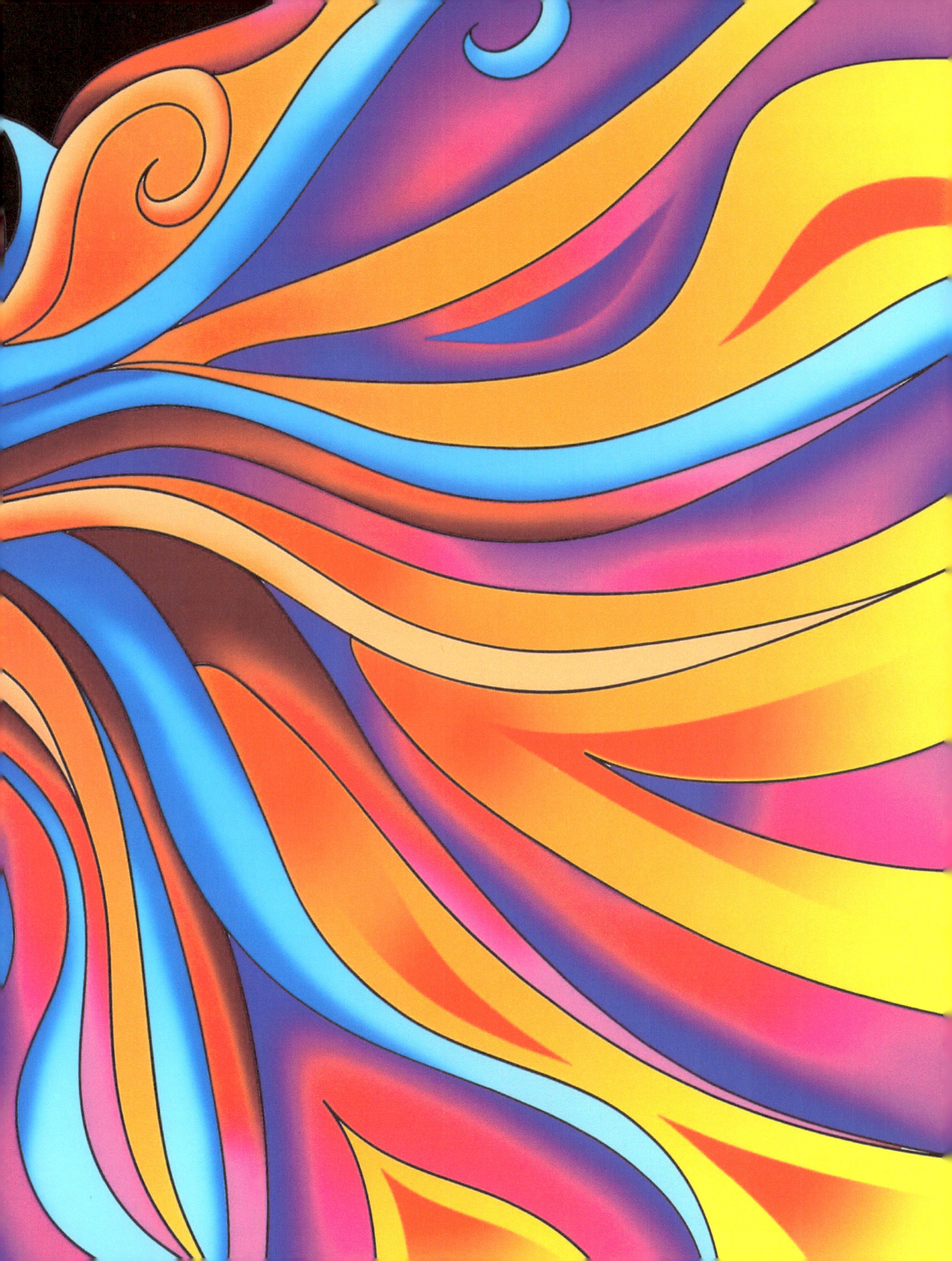

**For knowledge is limited.
Imagination embraces the entire world,
stimulating progress,
giving birth to evolution.**

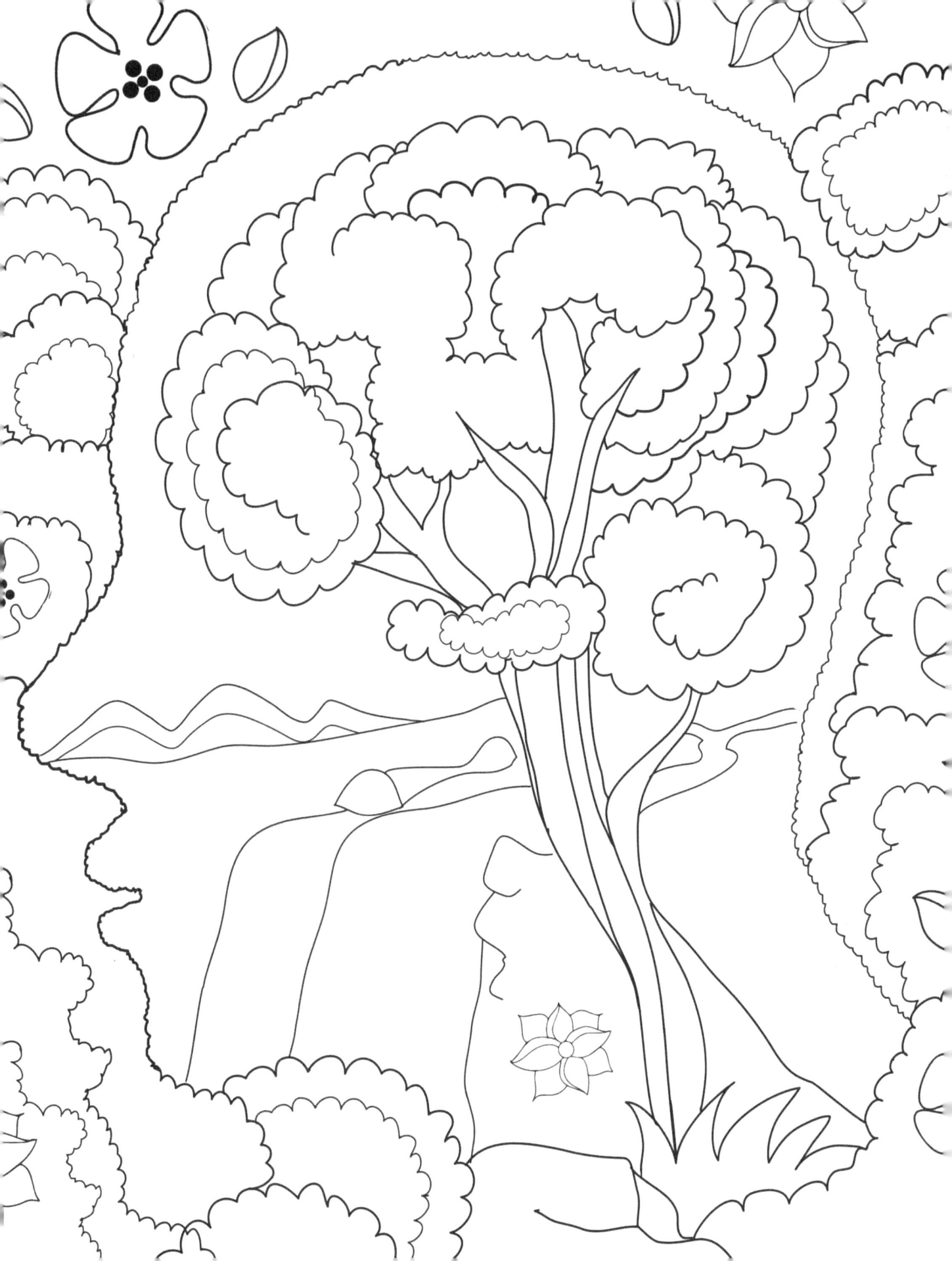

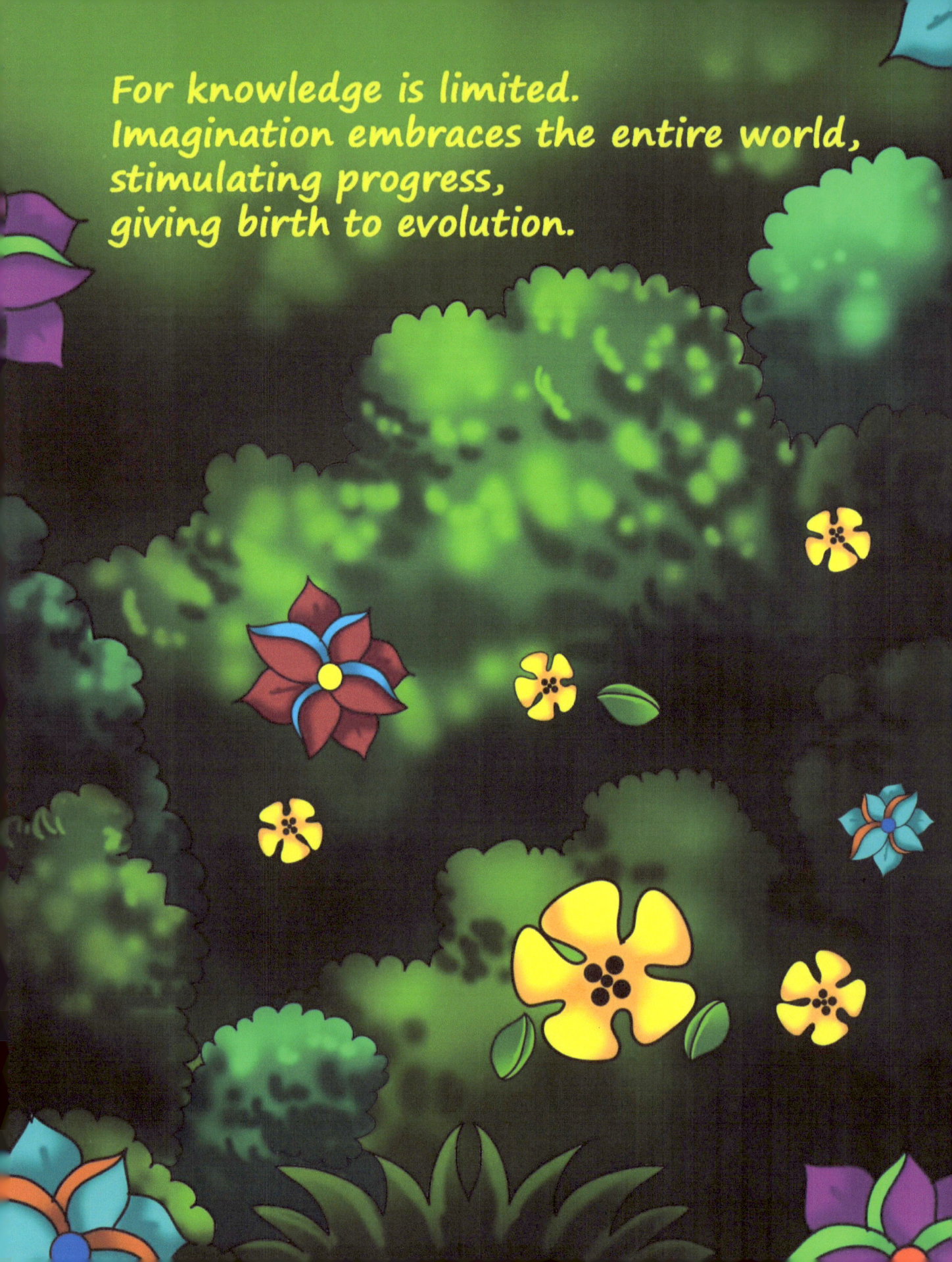

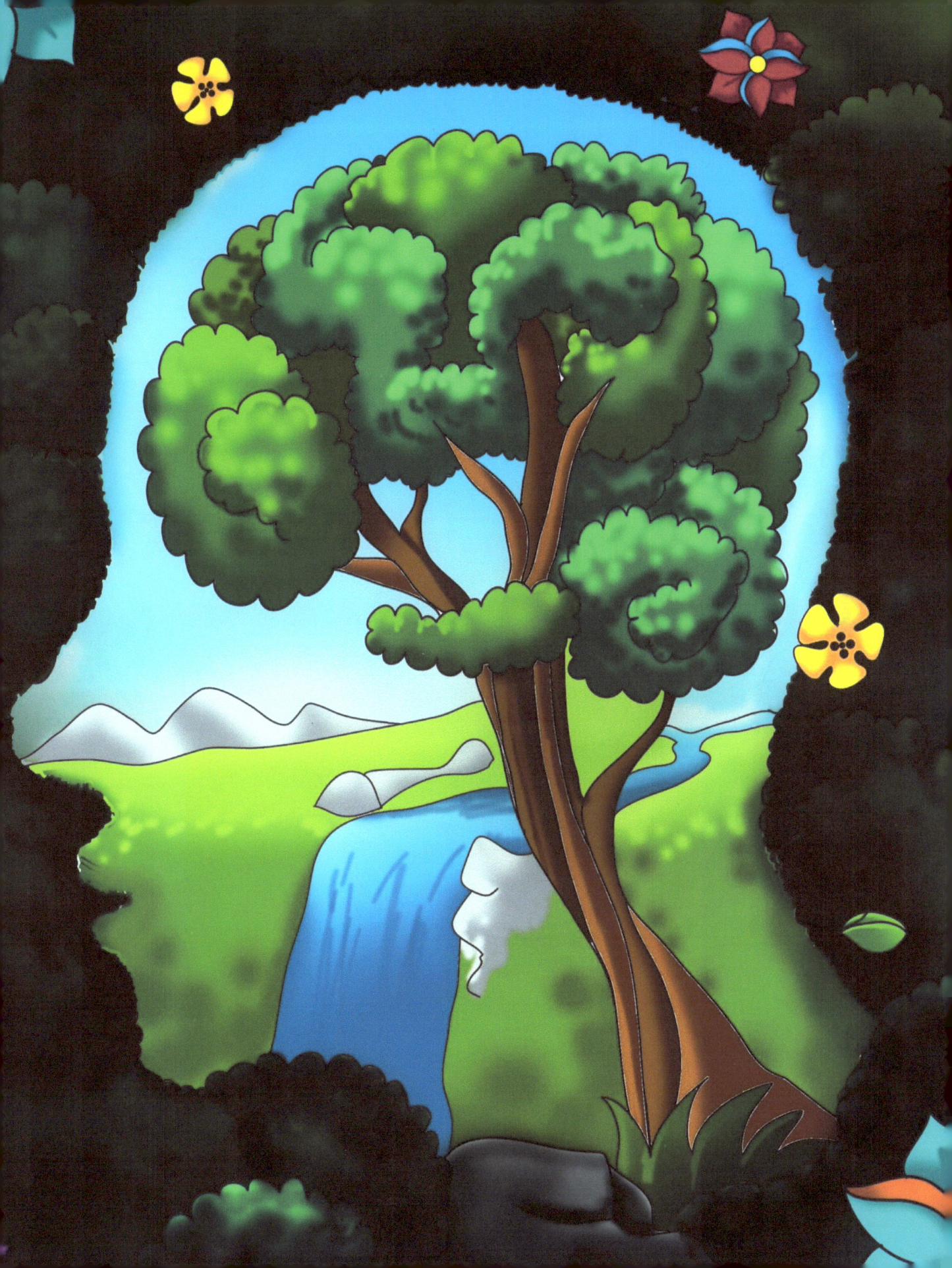

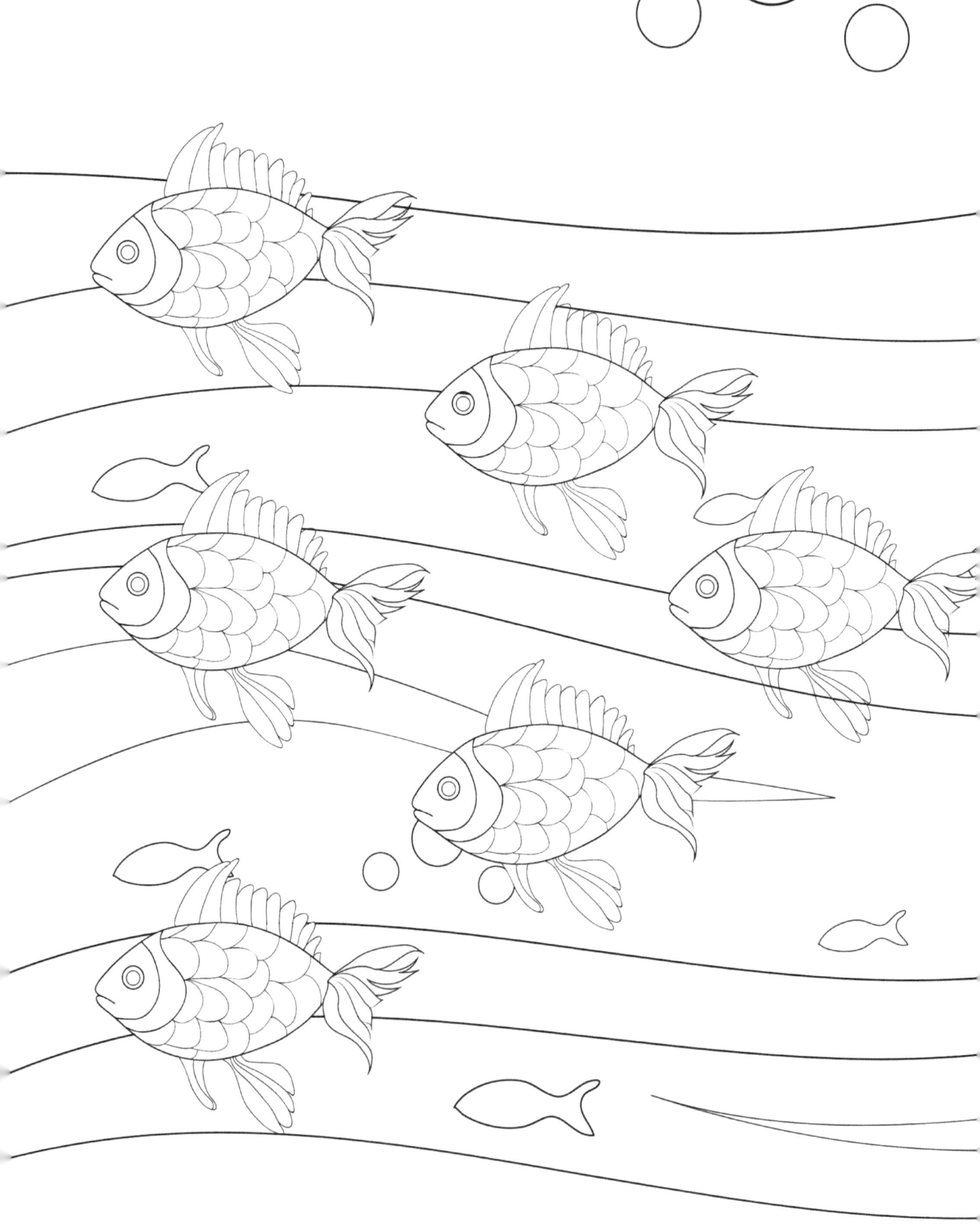

I am not suggesting, knowledge is meaningless, I am suggesting that knowledge is less important than thinking for yourself.

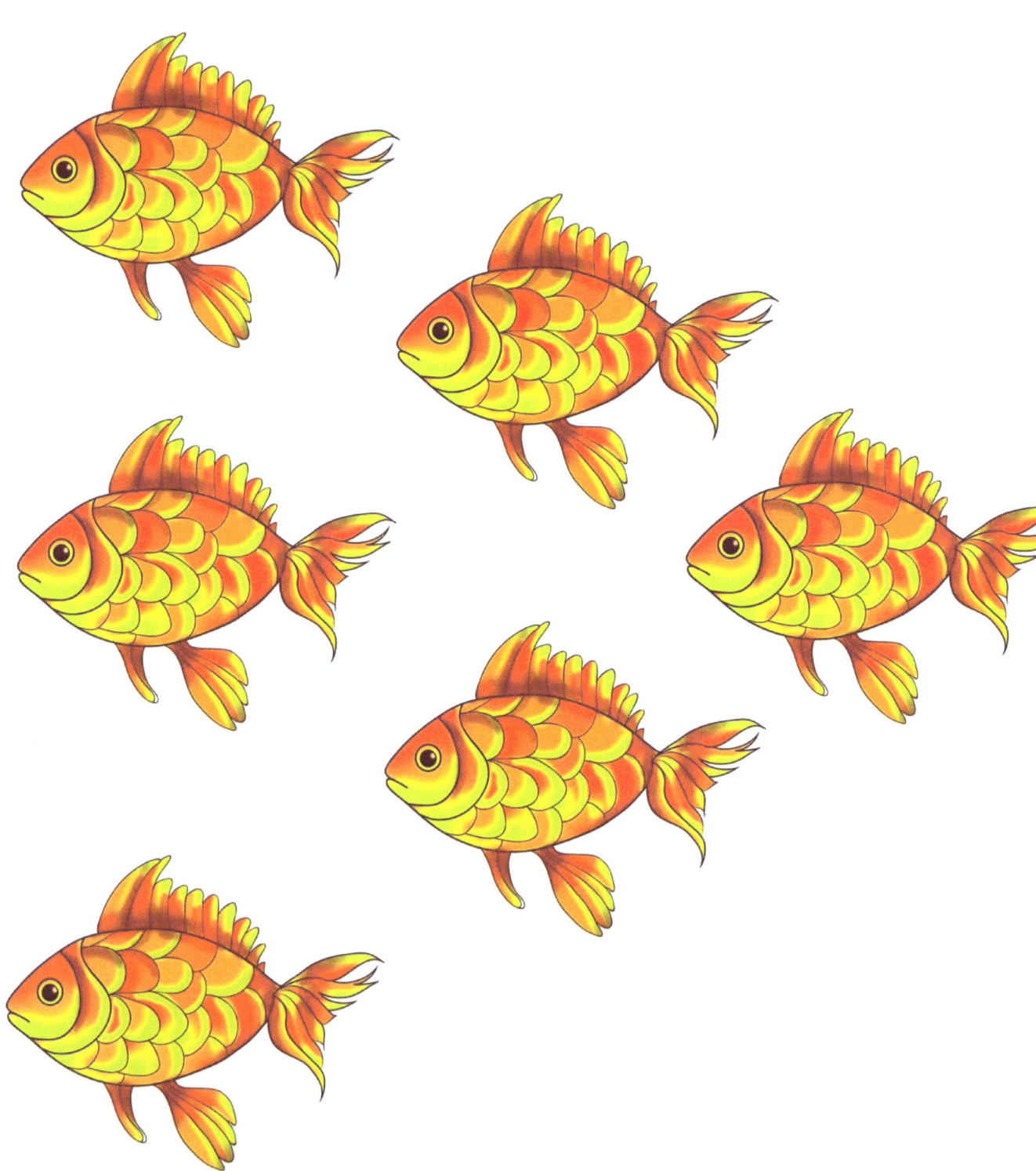

I am not suggesting, knowledge is meaningless, I am suggesting that knowledge is less important than thinking for yourself.

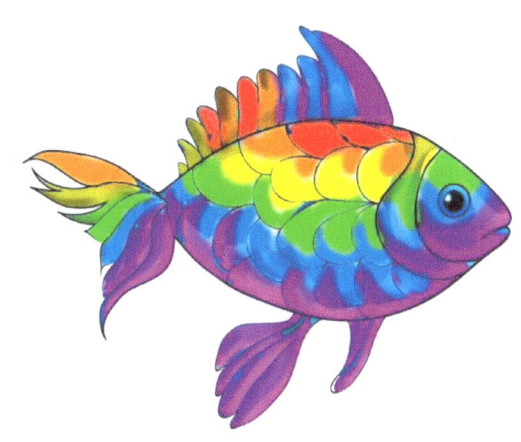

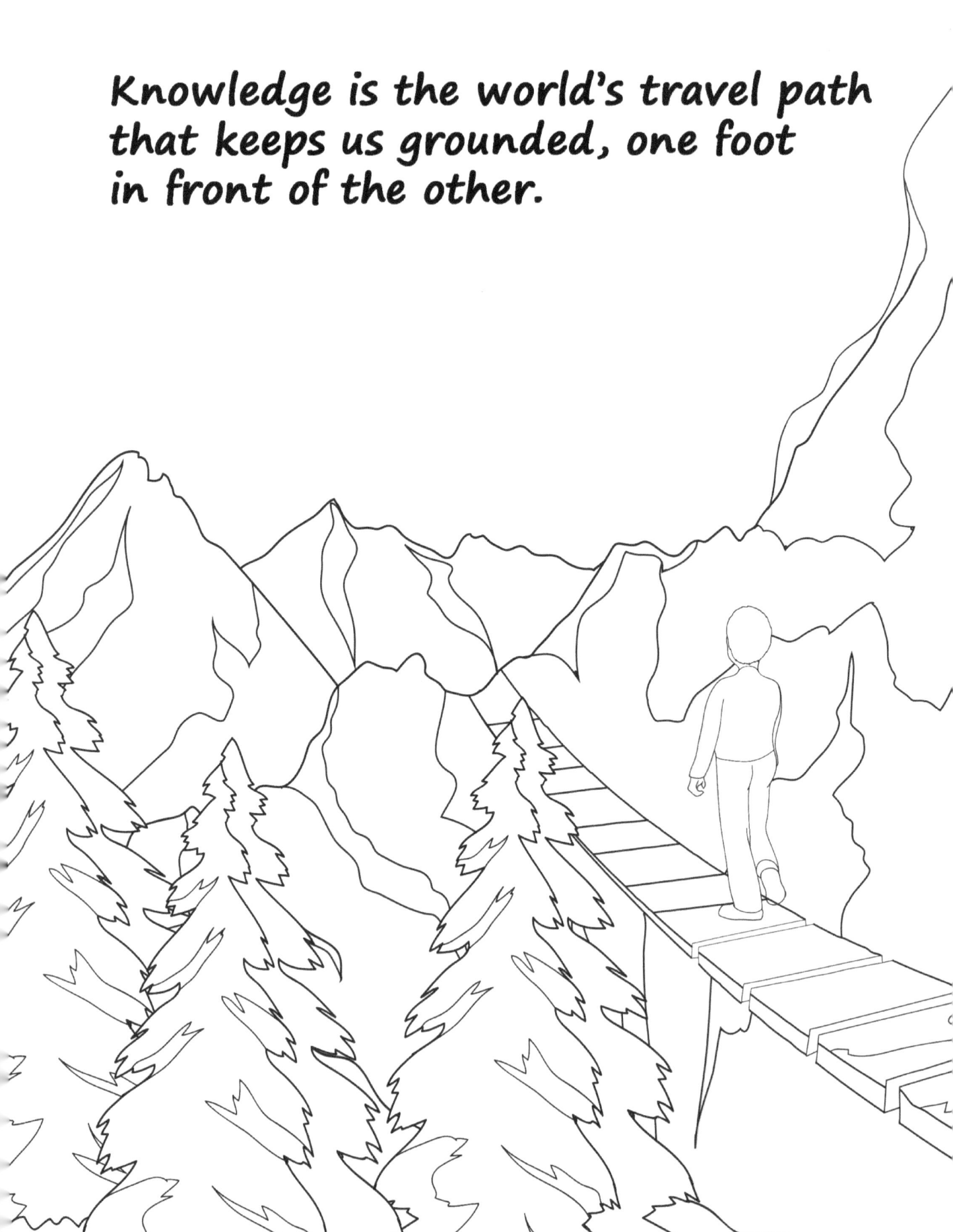
Knowledge is the world's travel path that keeps us grounded, one foot in front of the other.

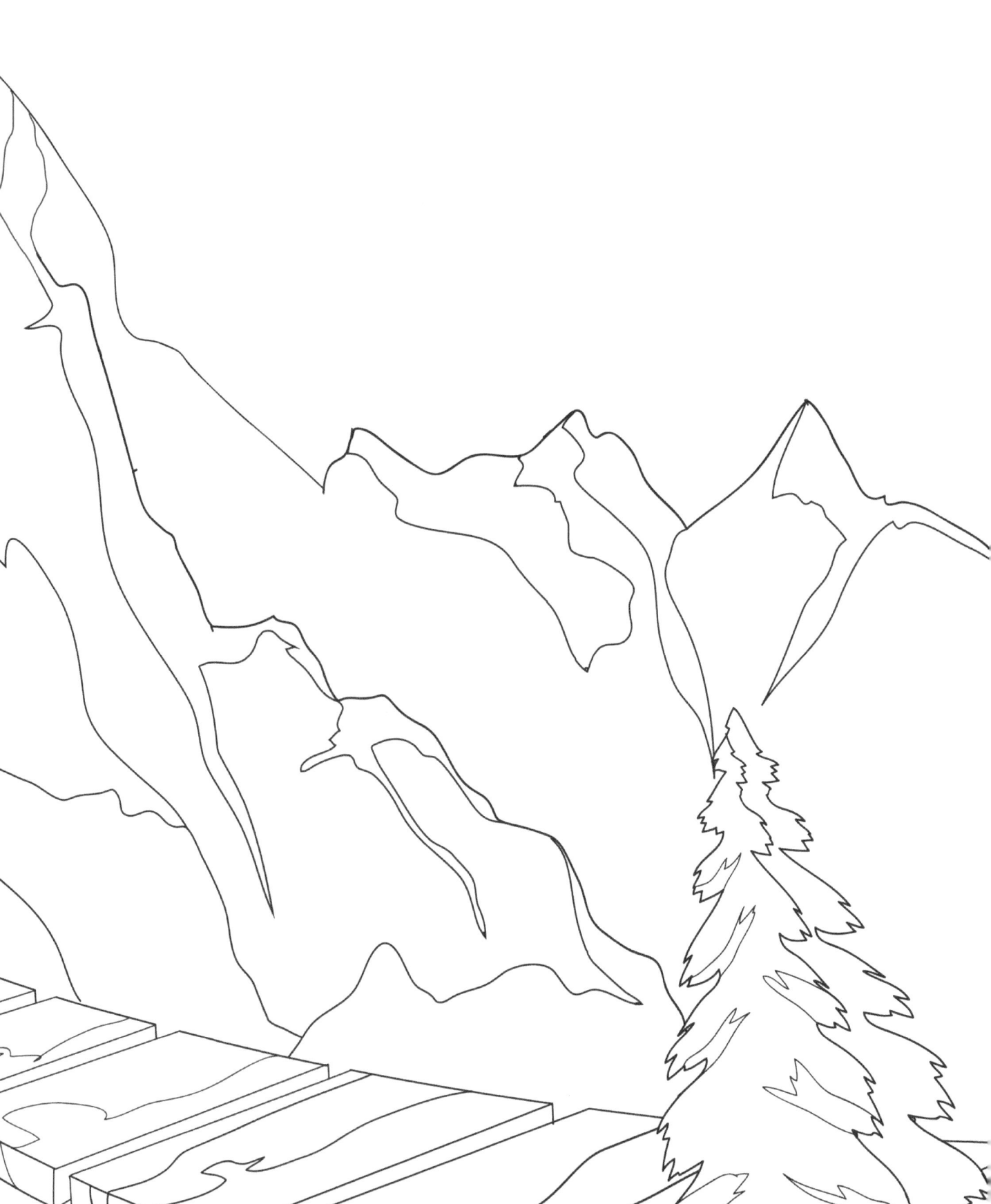

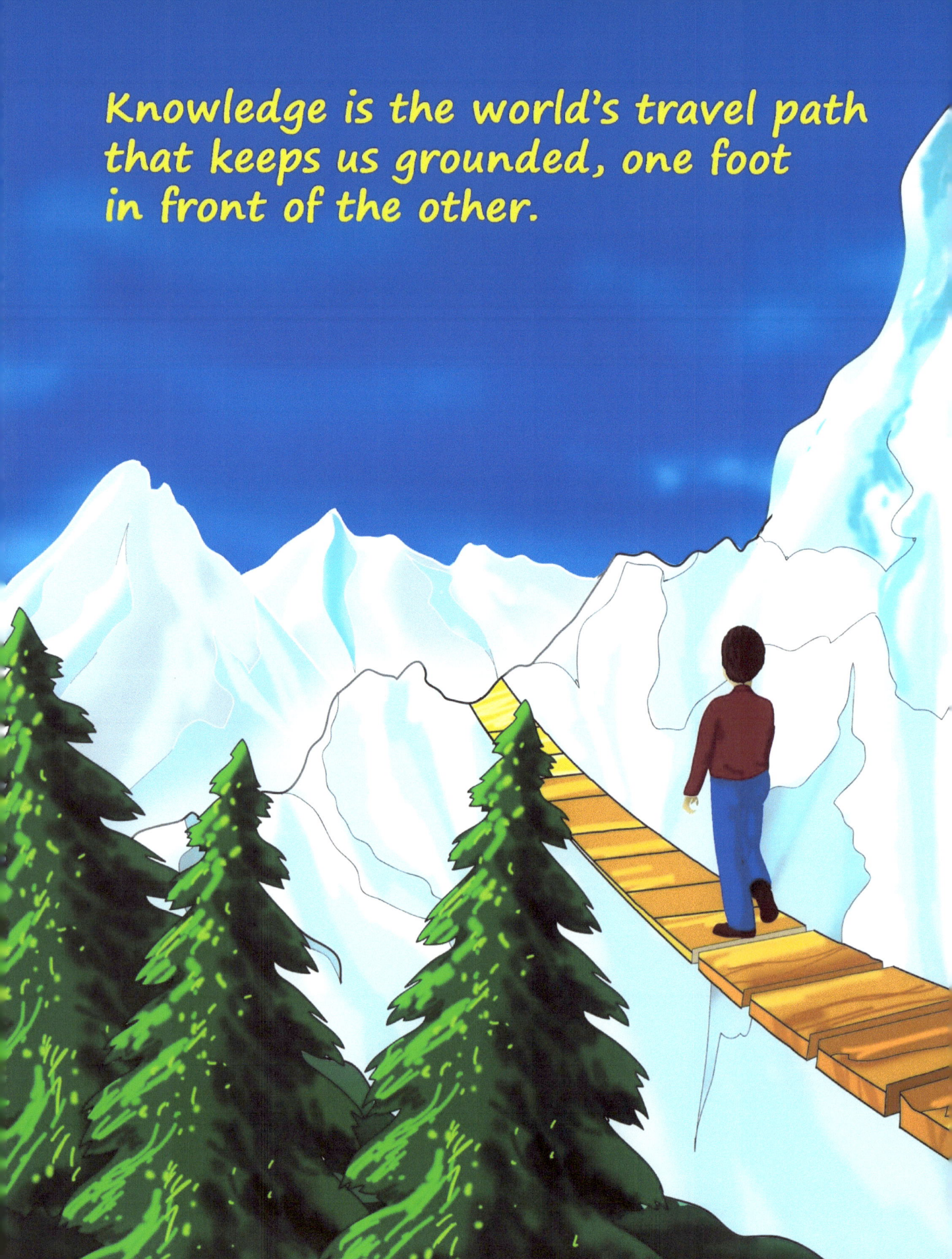

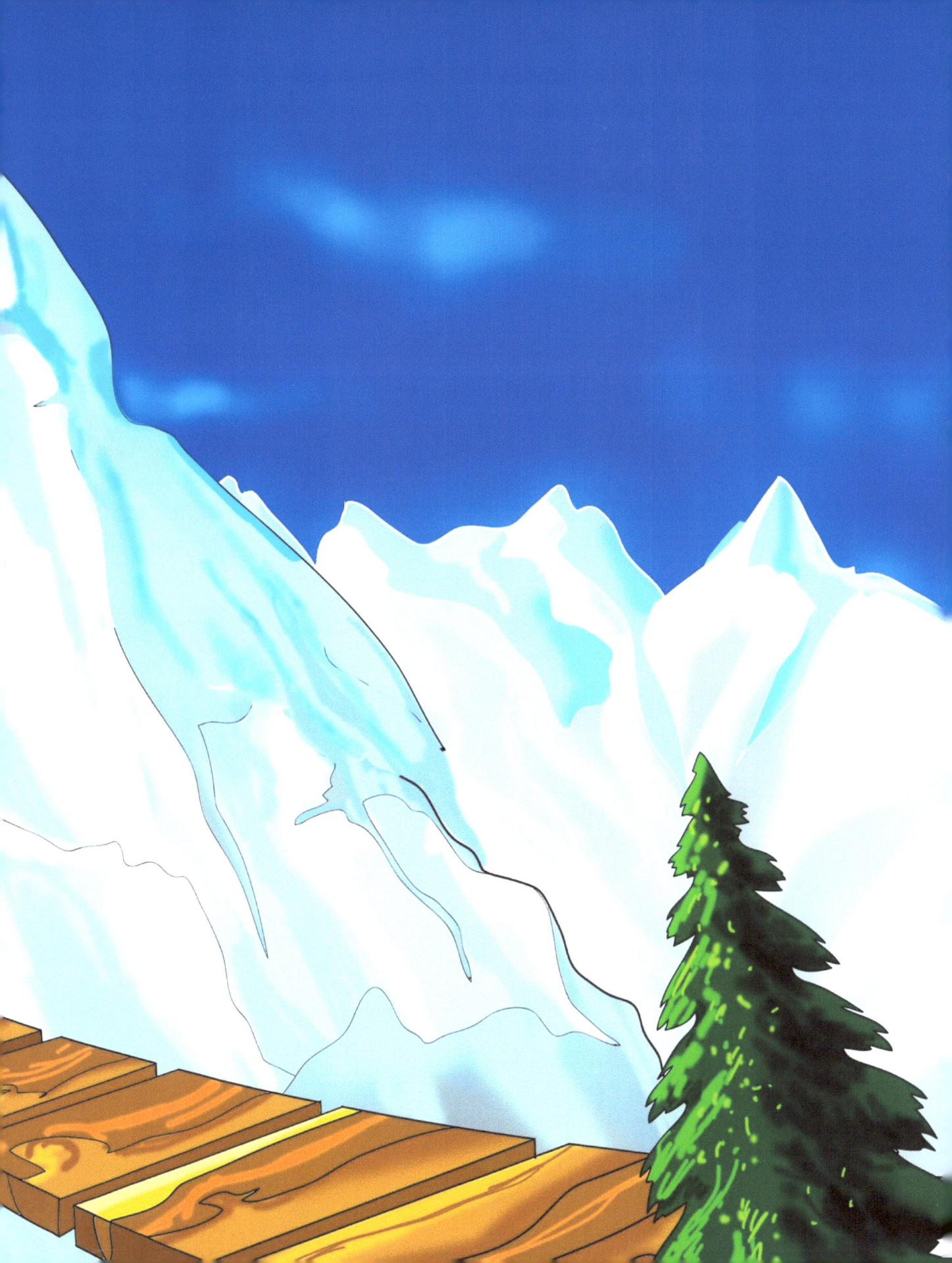

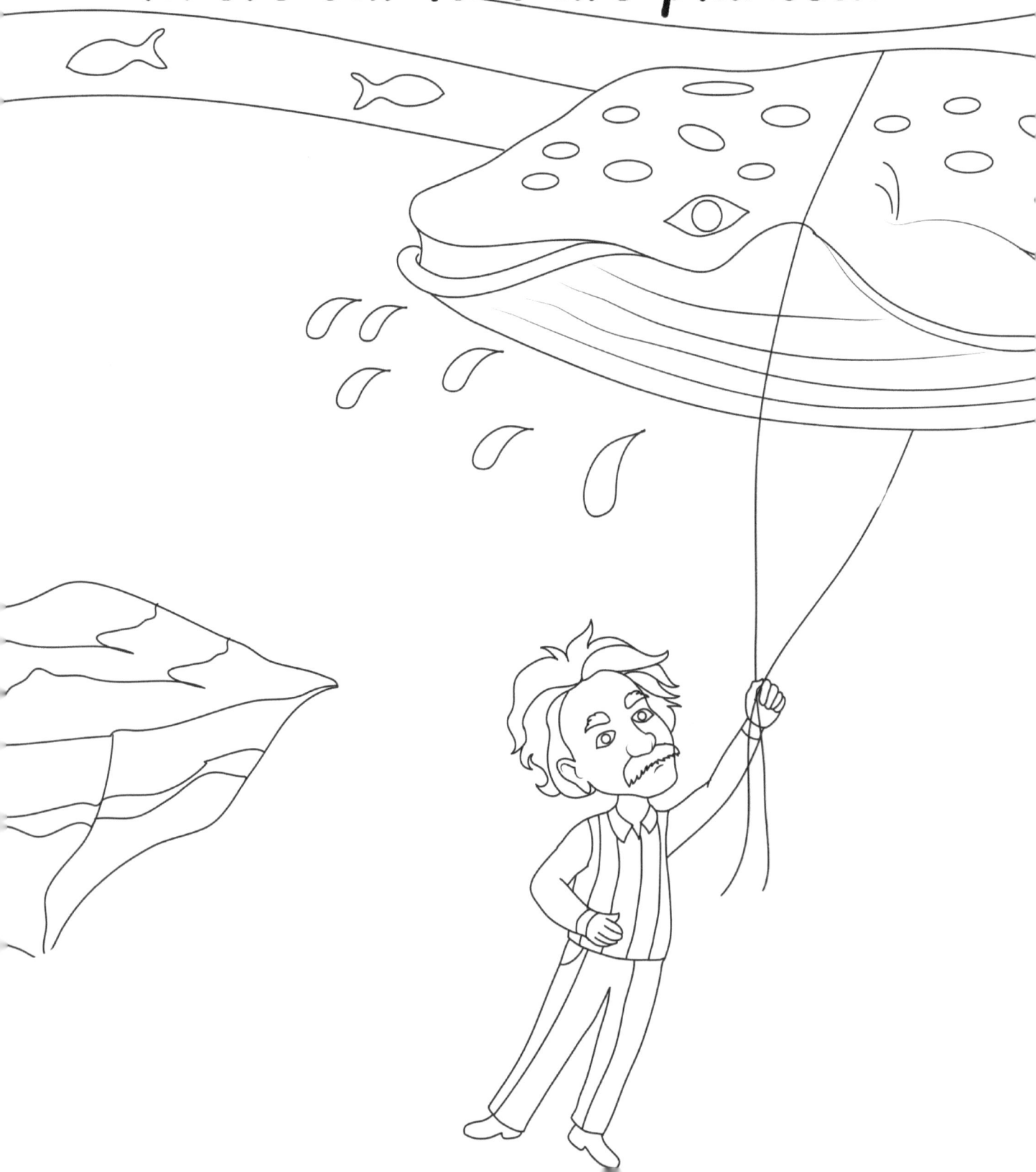

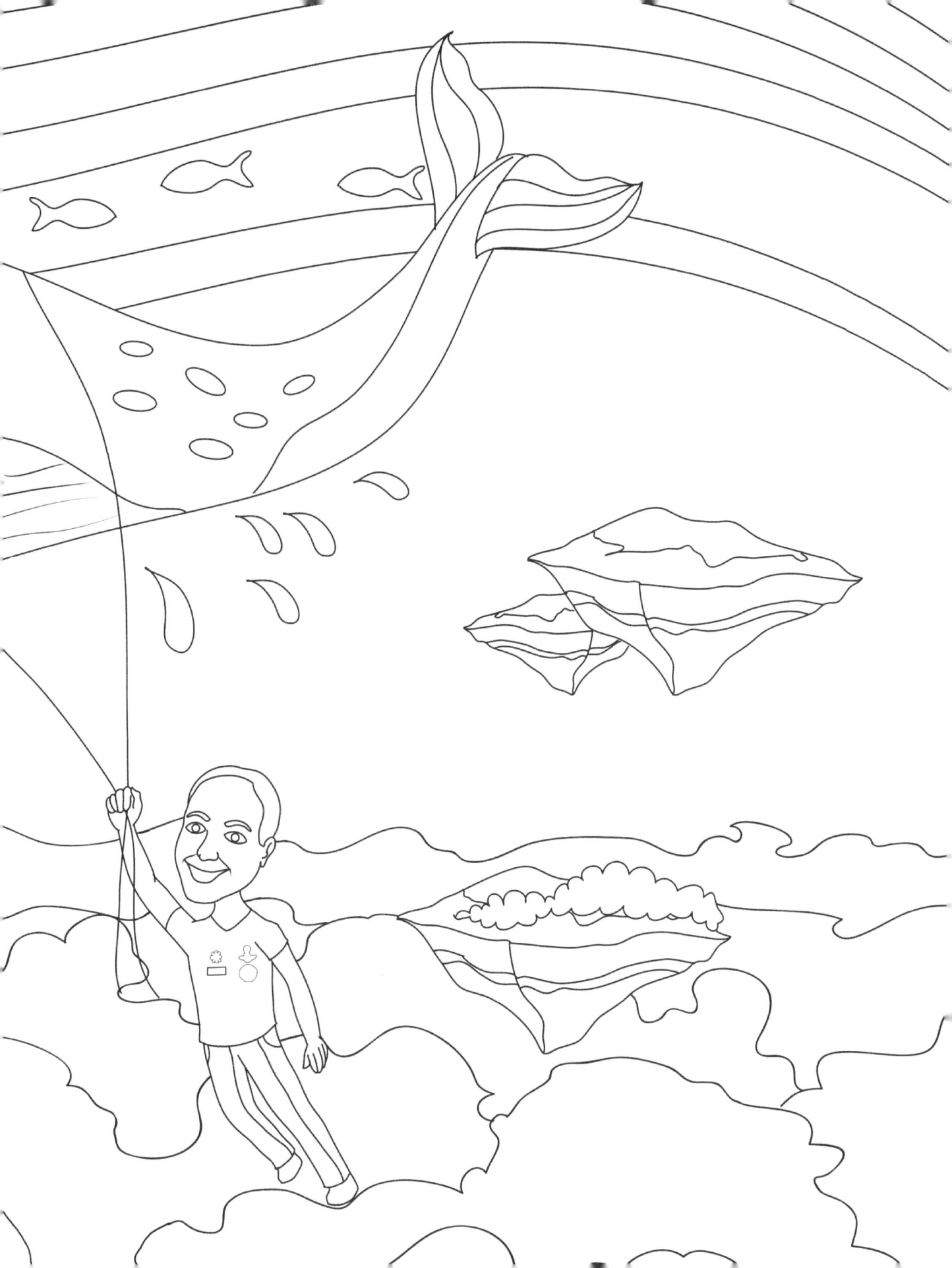

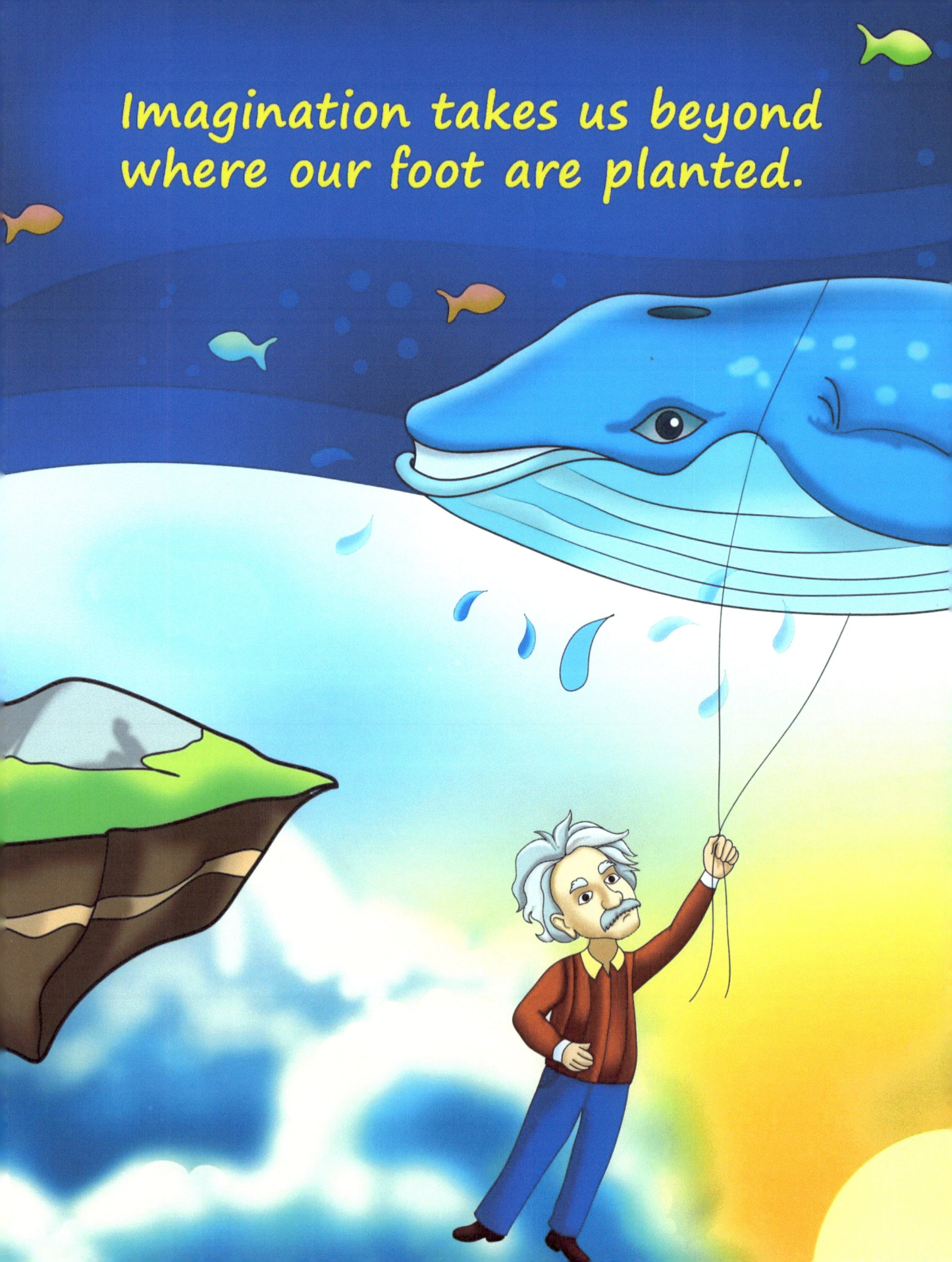

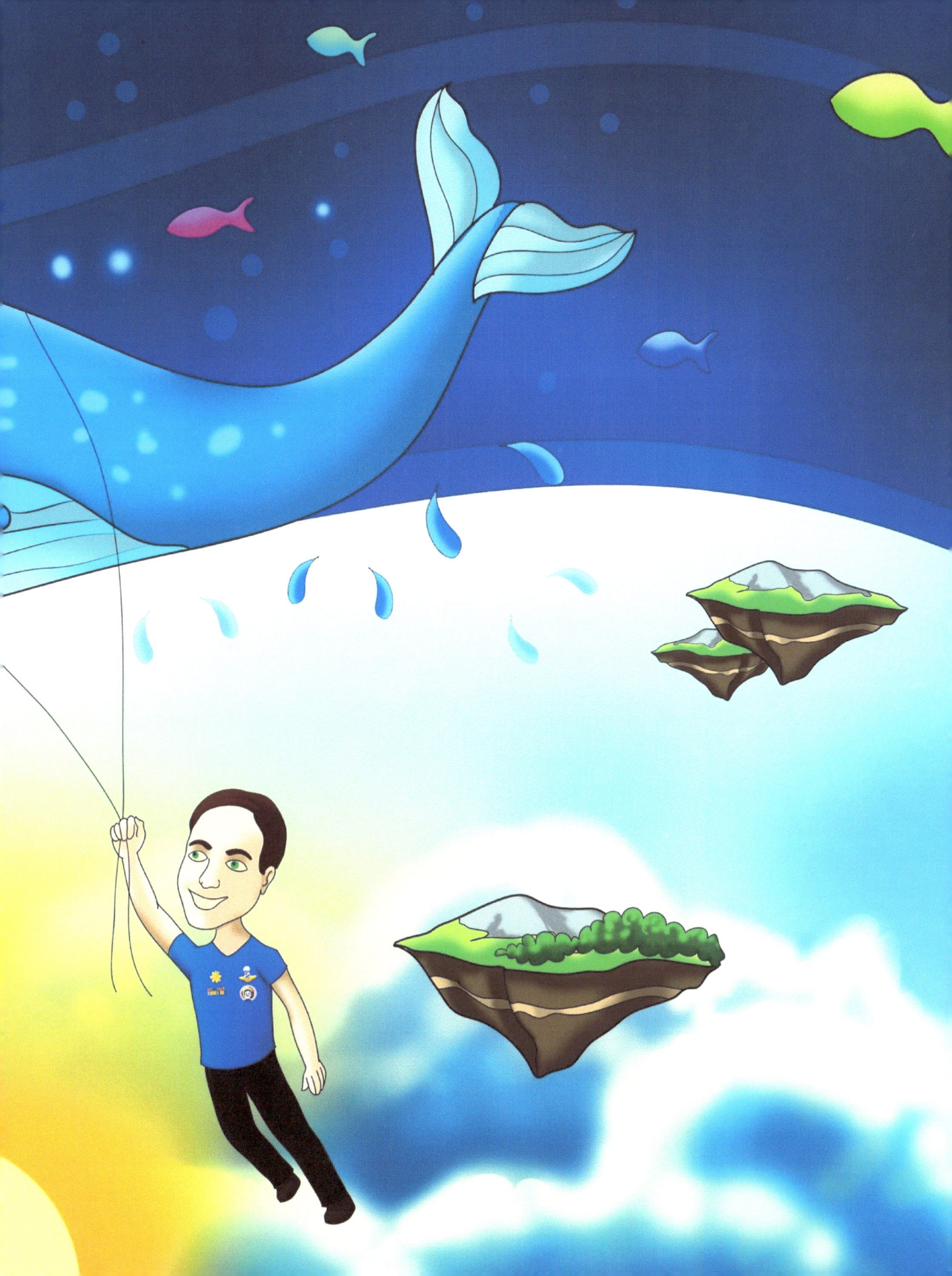

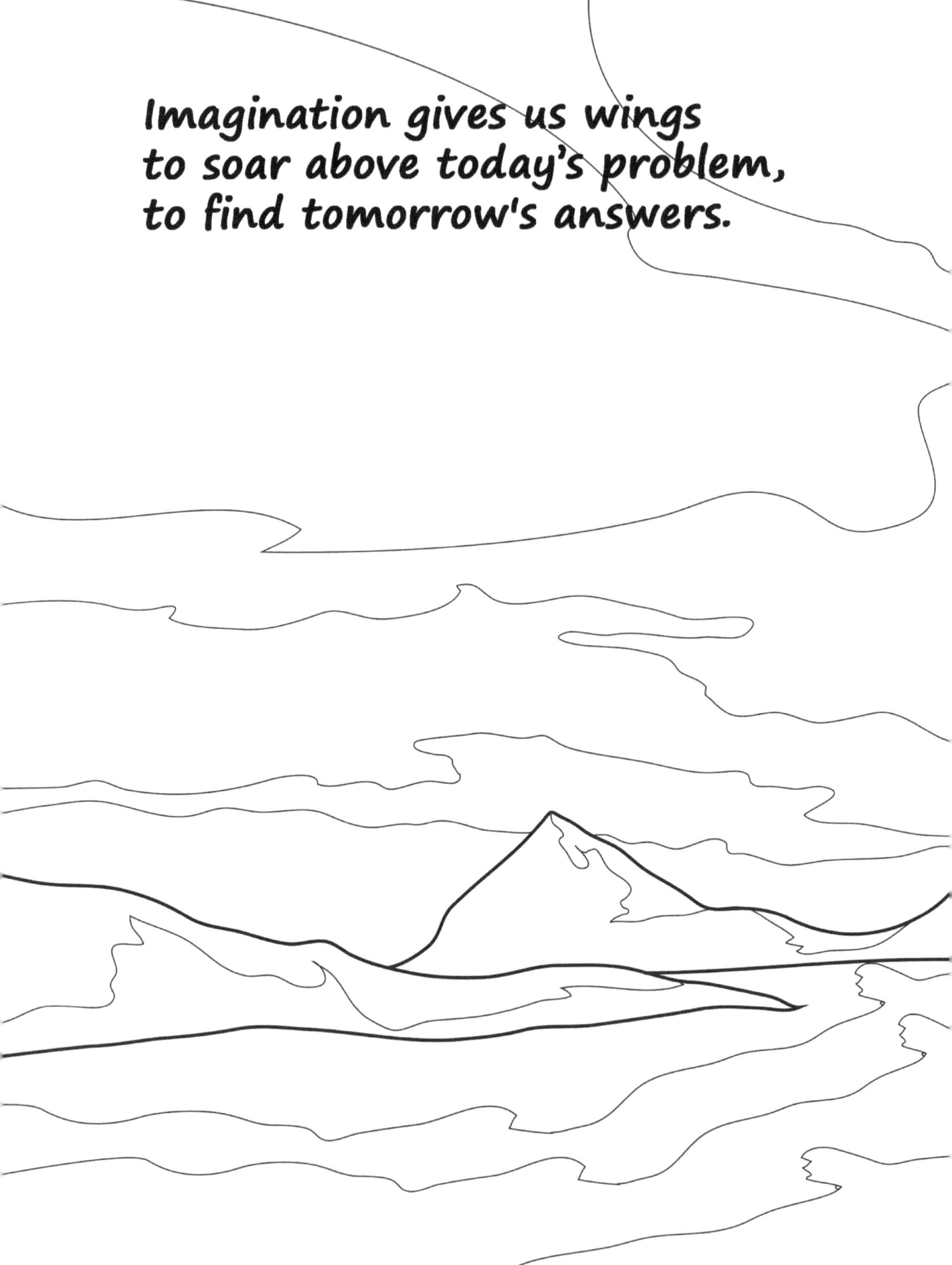

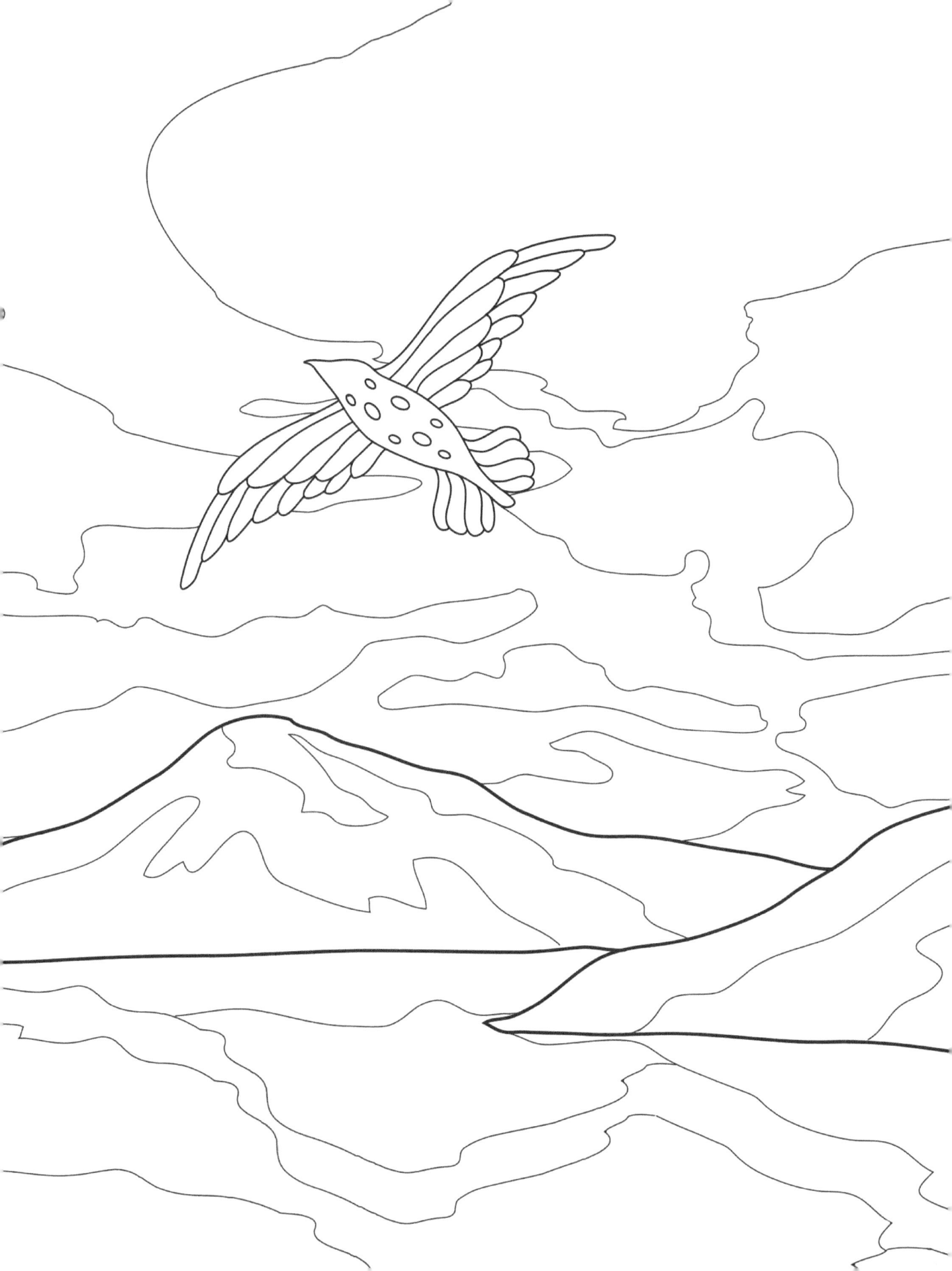

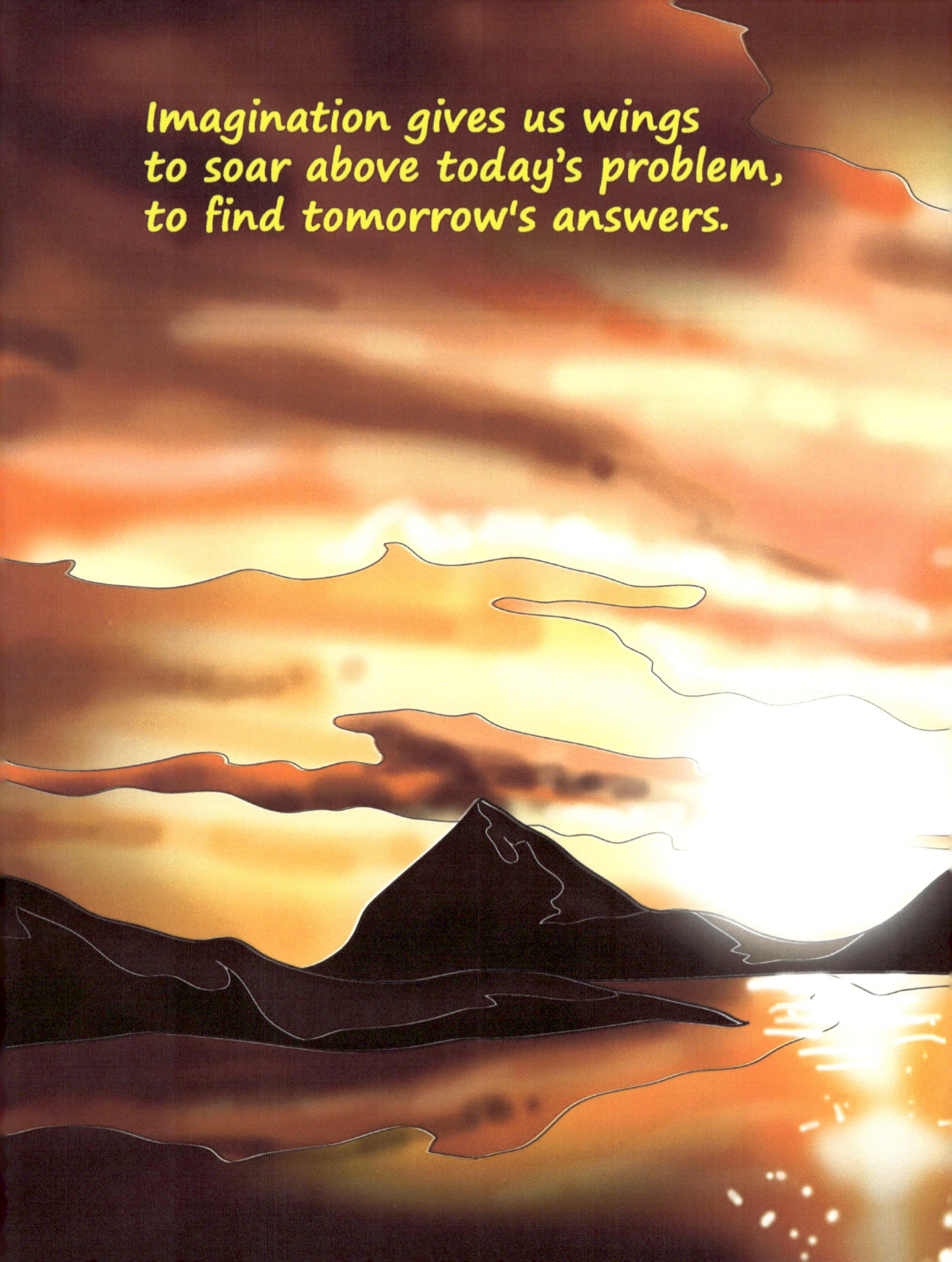

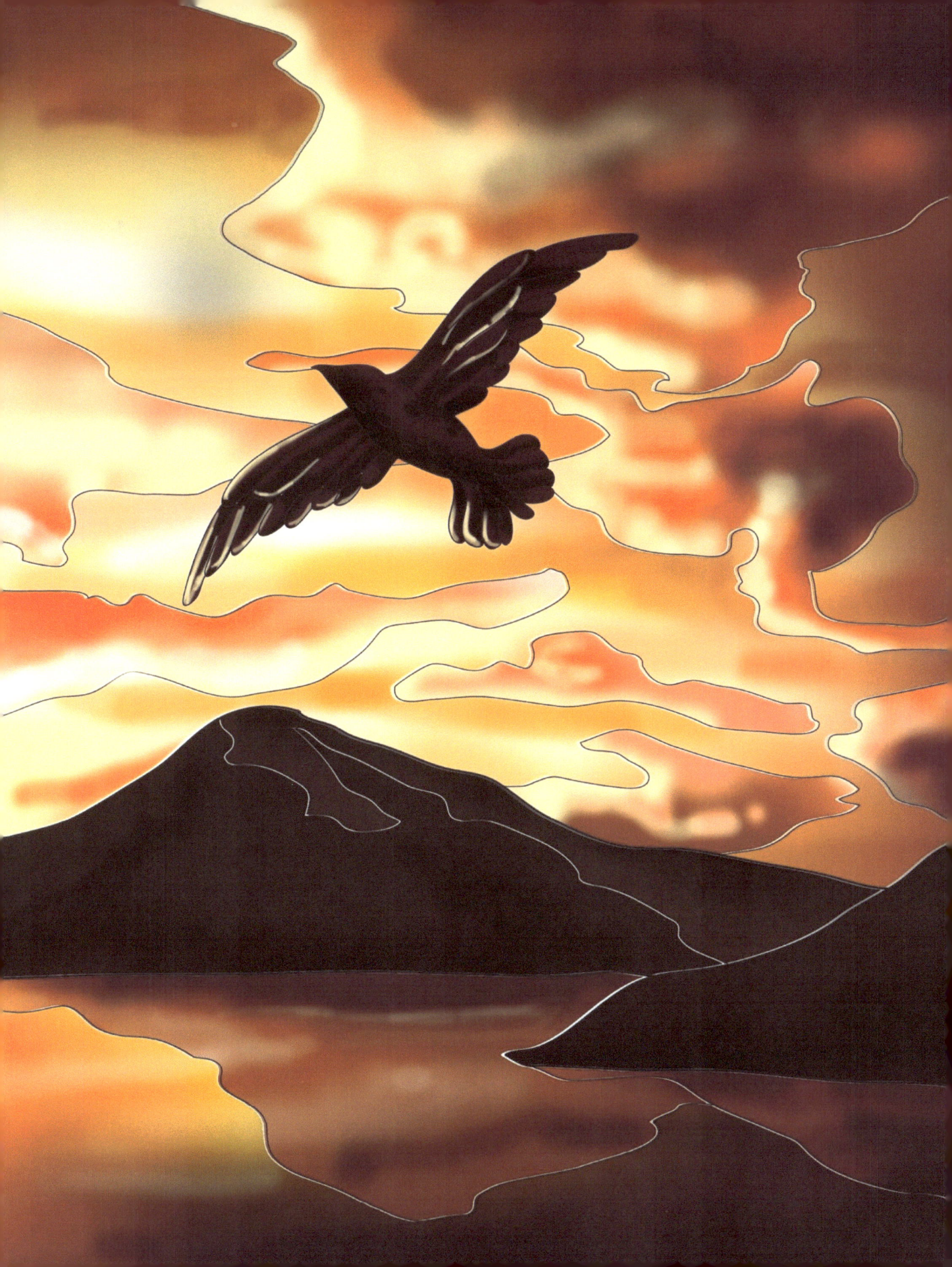

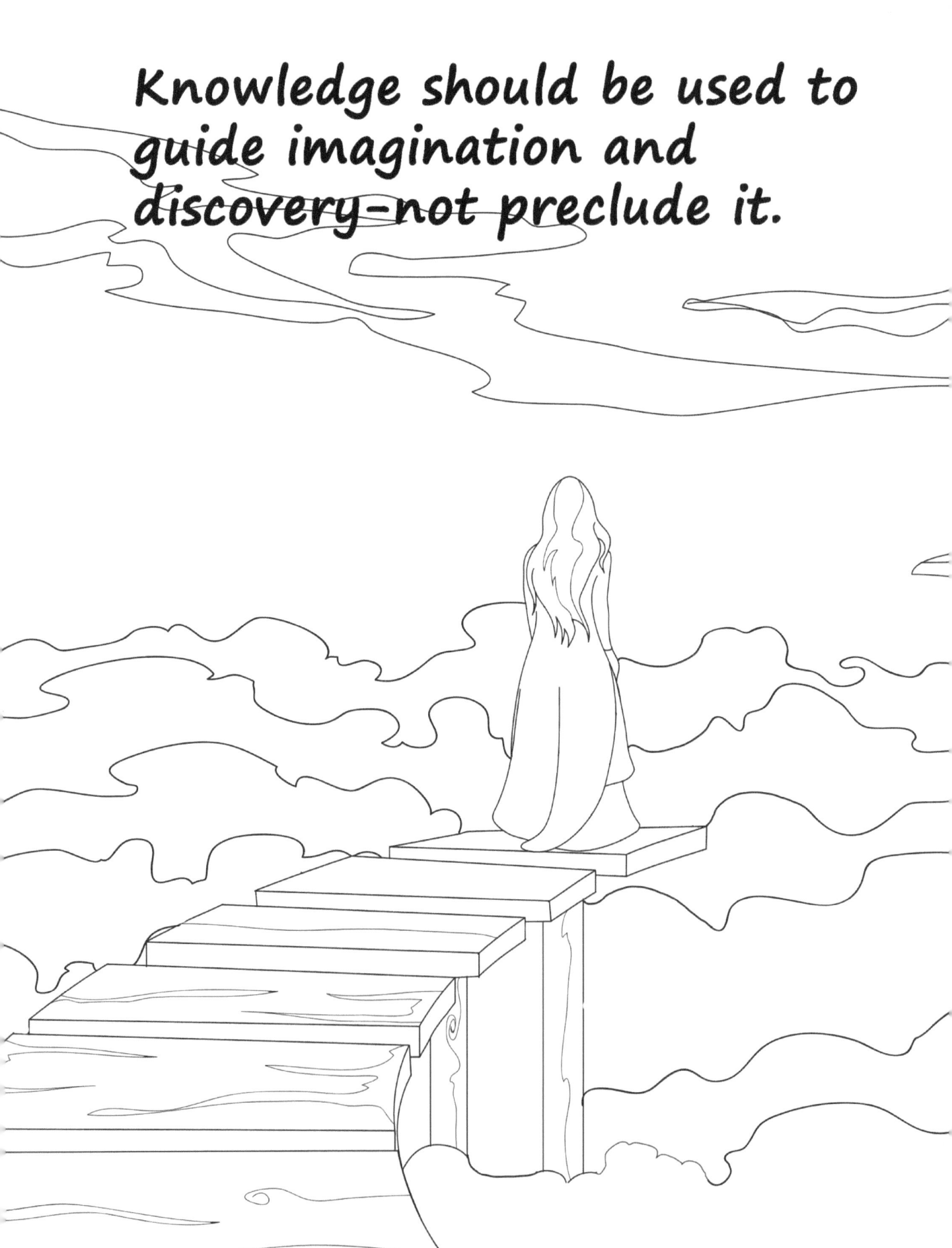

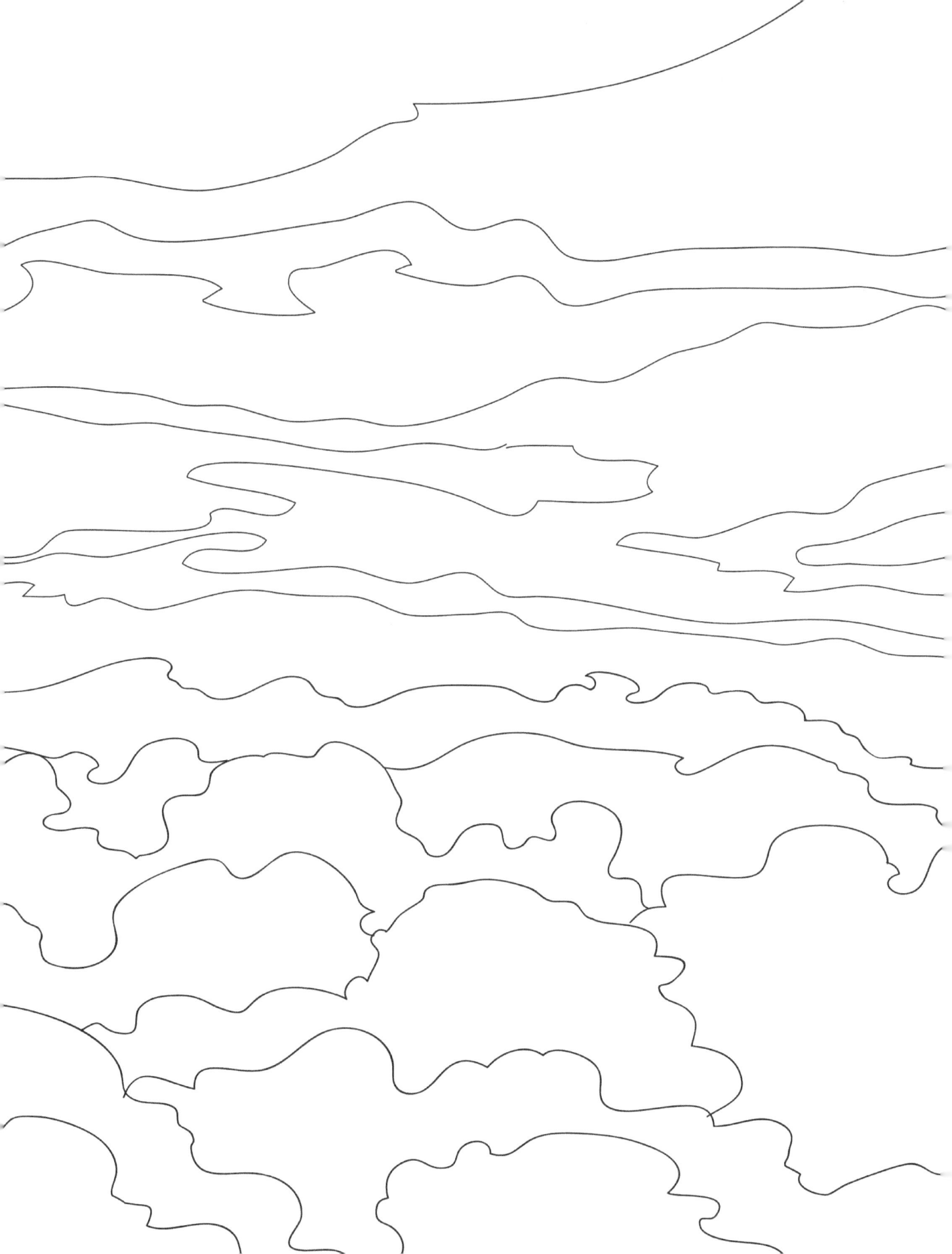

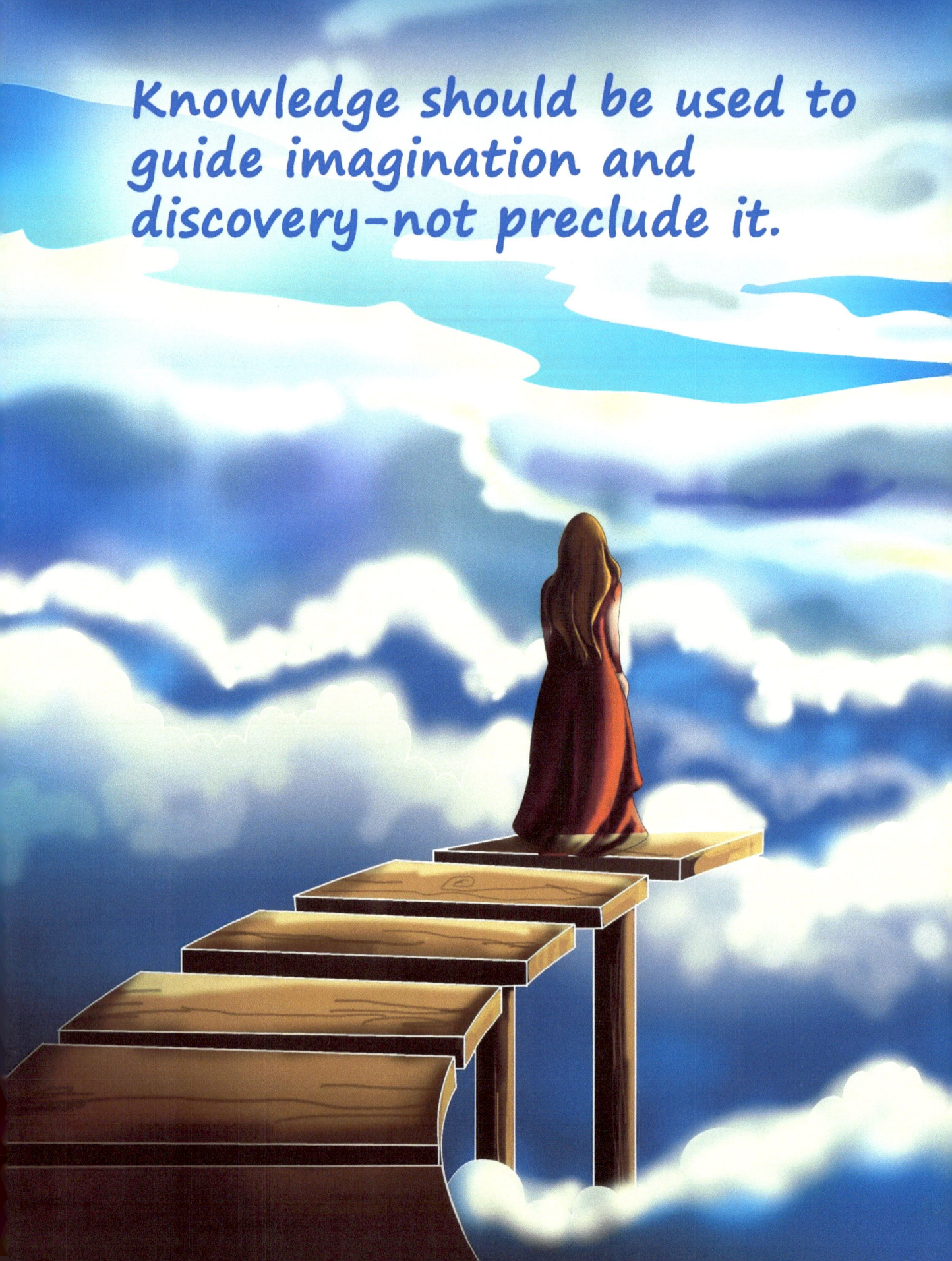

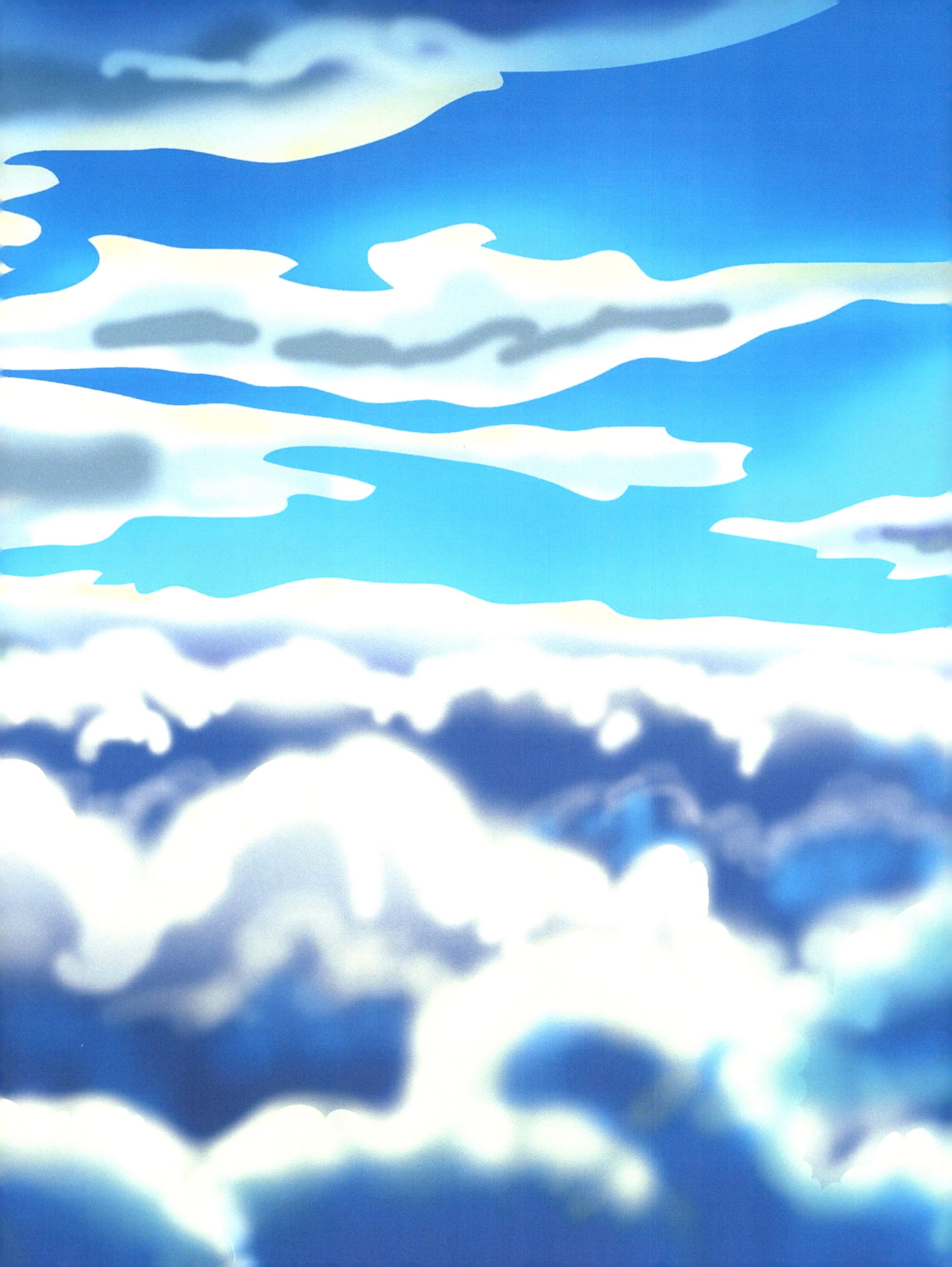

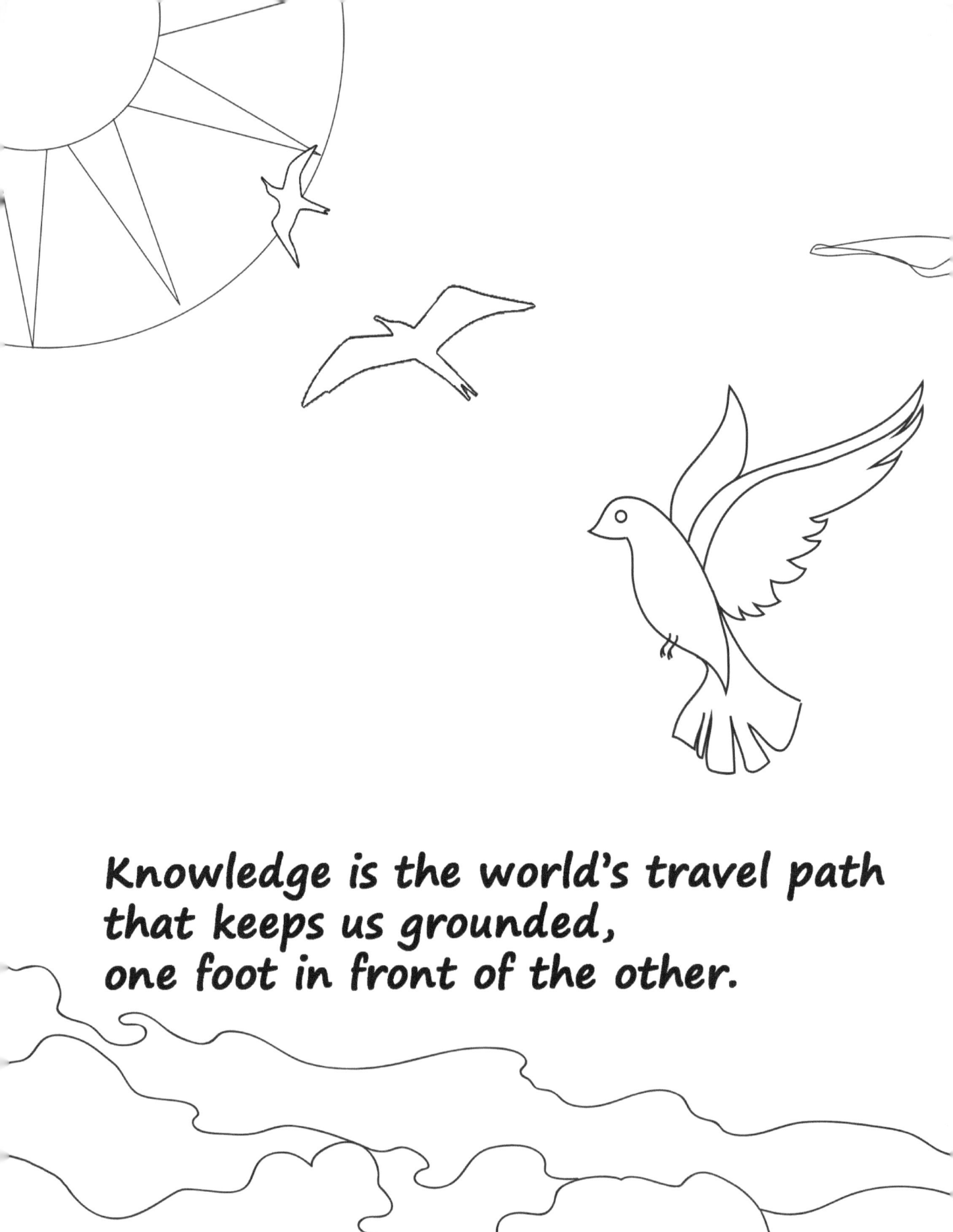

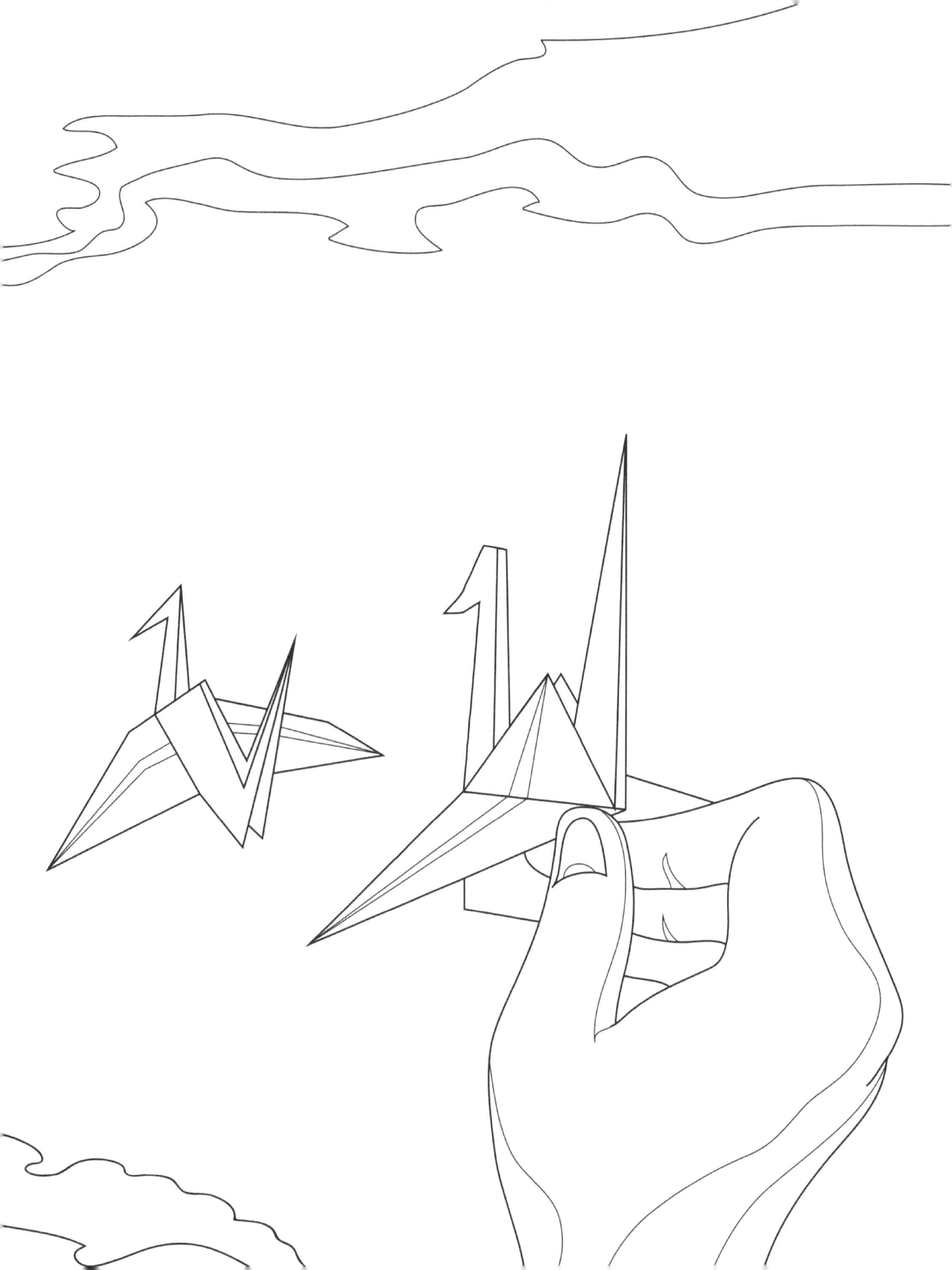

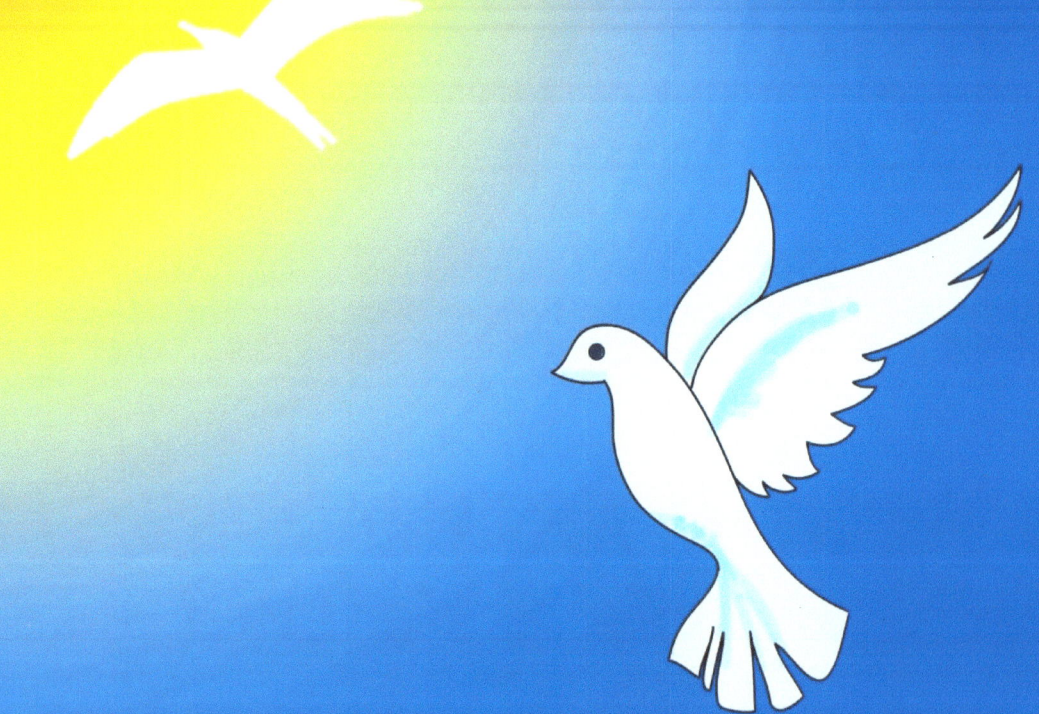

Knowledge is the world's travel path that keeps us grounded, one foot in front of the other.

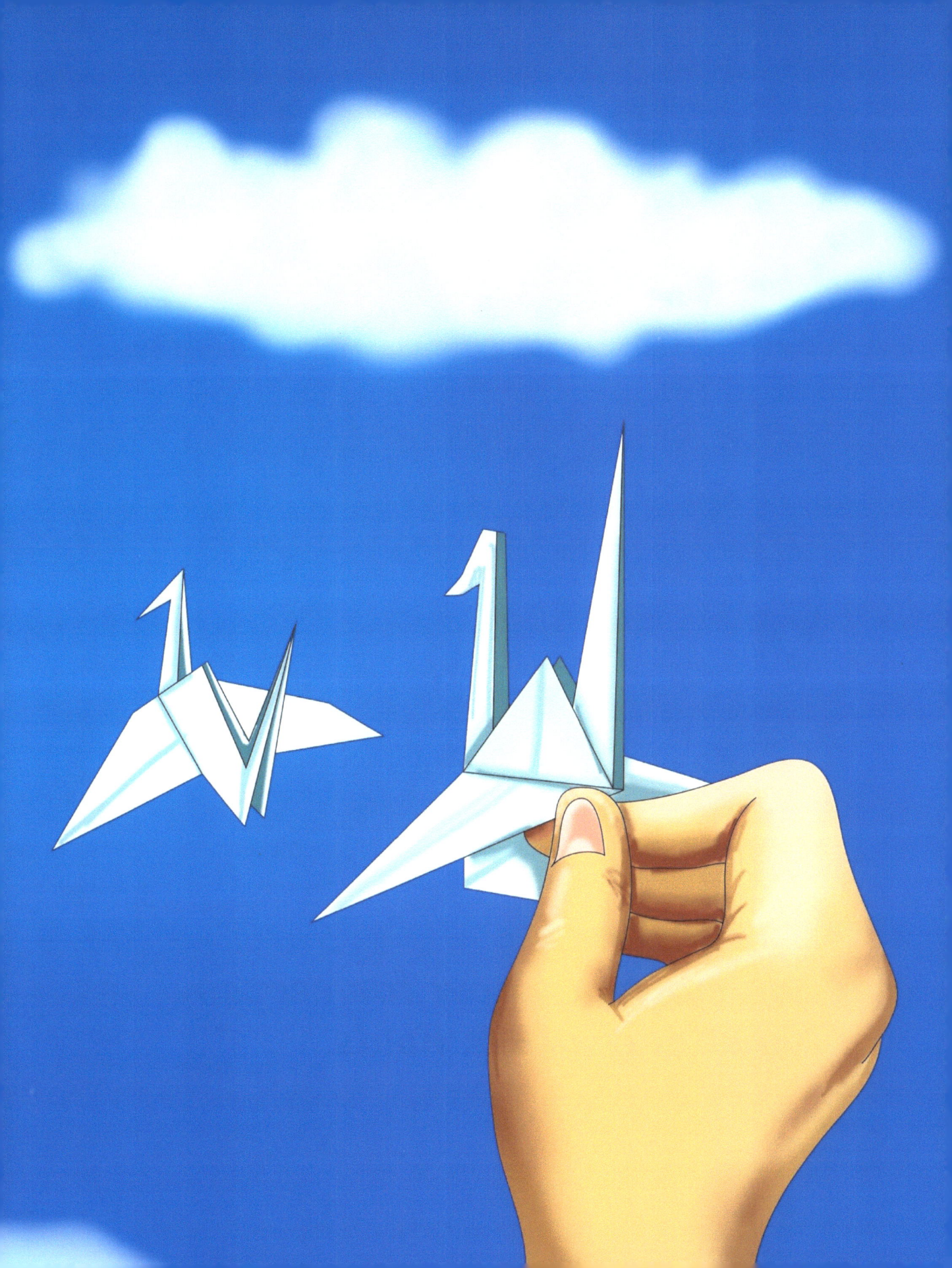

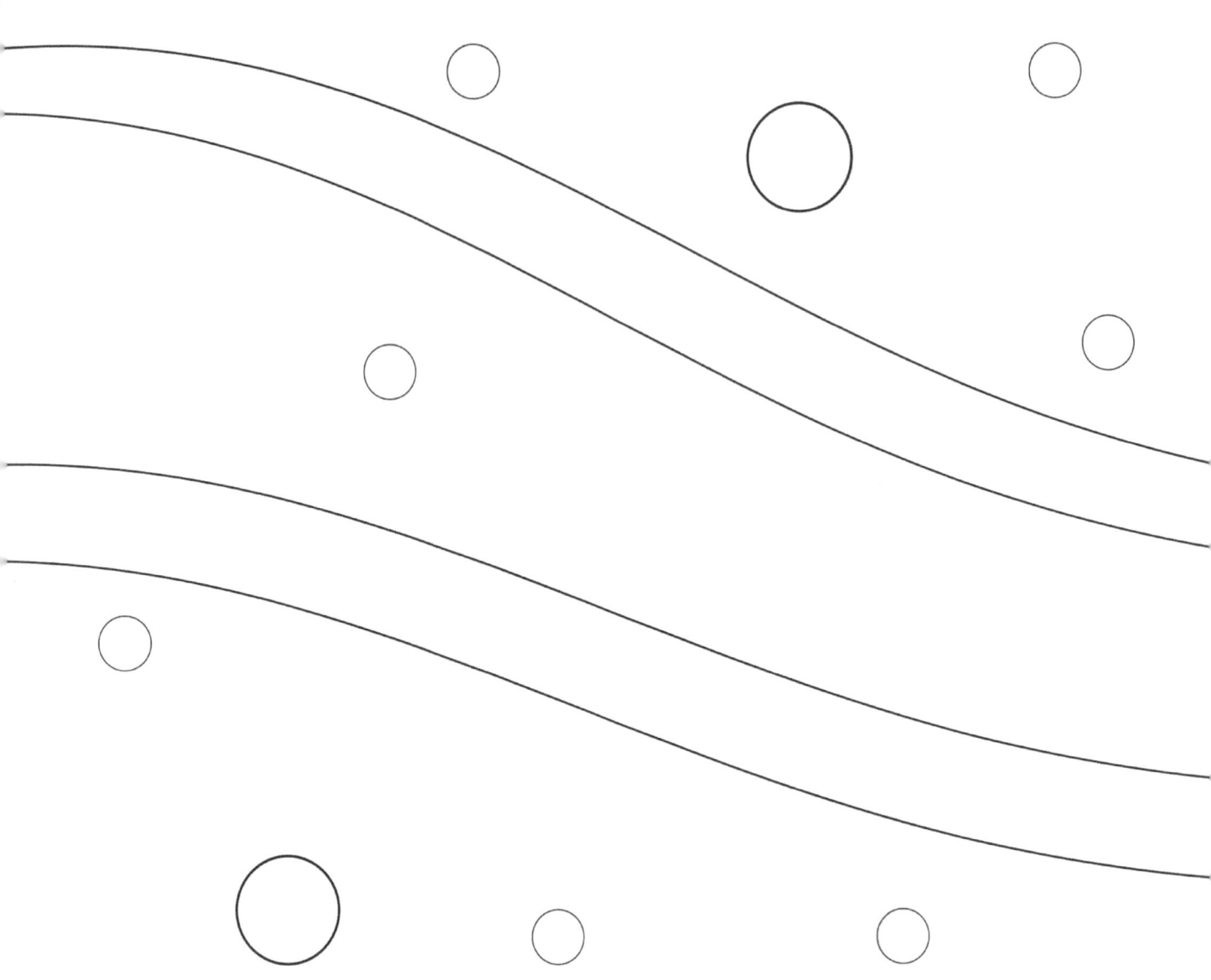

We can not know for certain what the future holds.

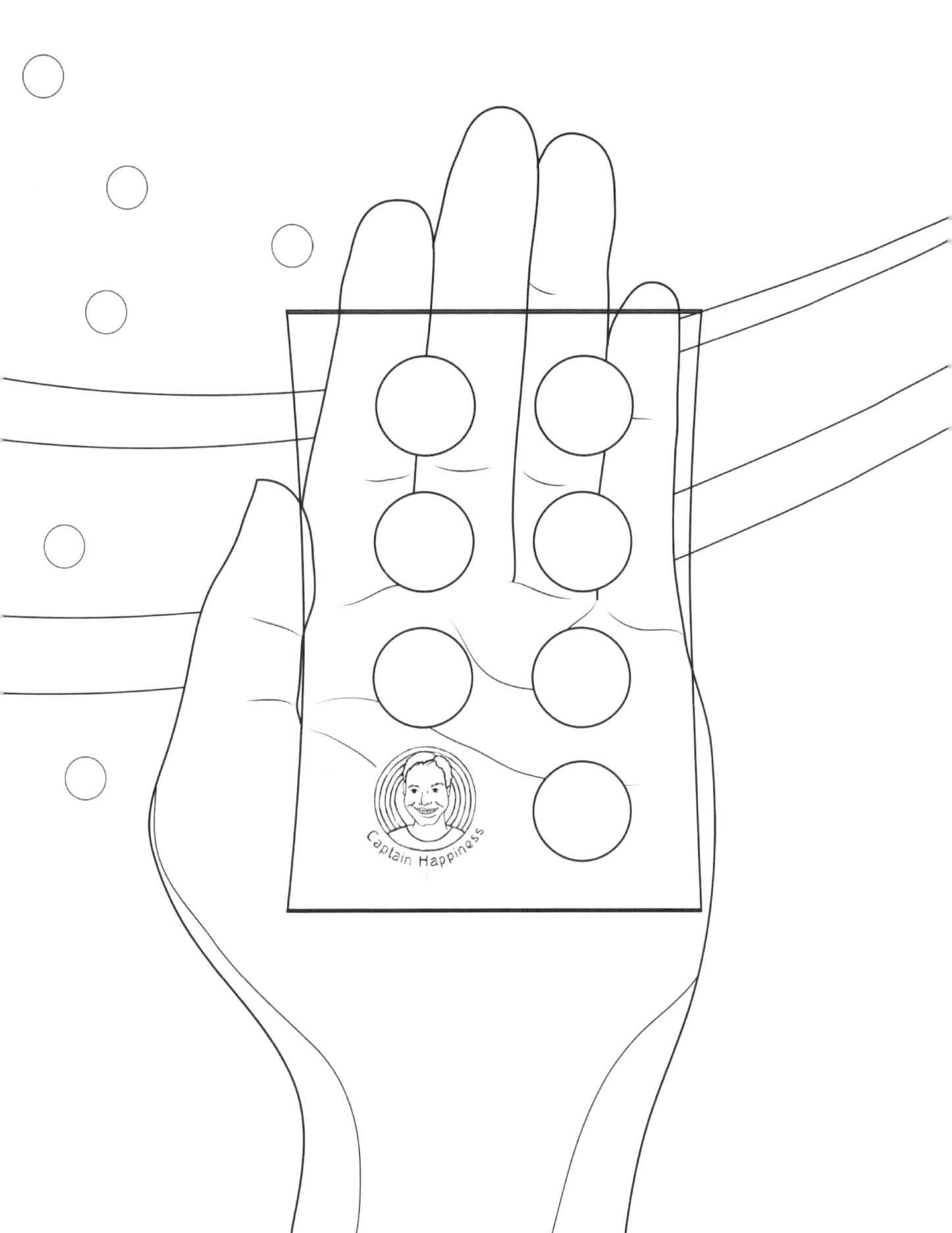

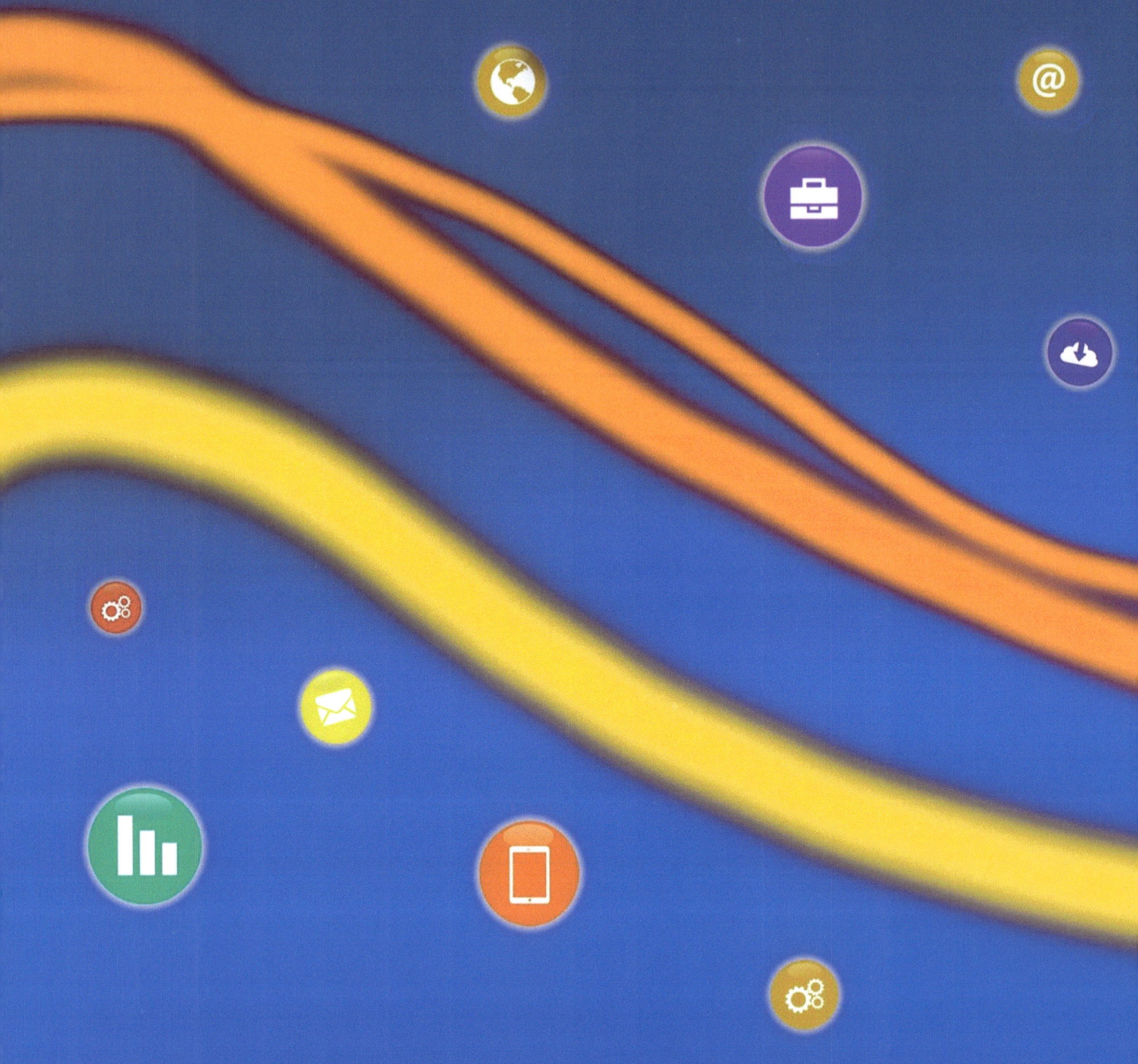

We can not know for certain what the future holds.

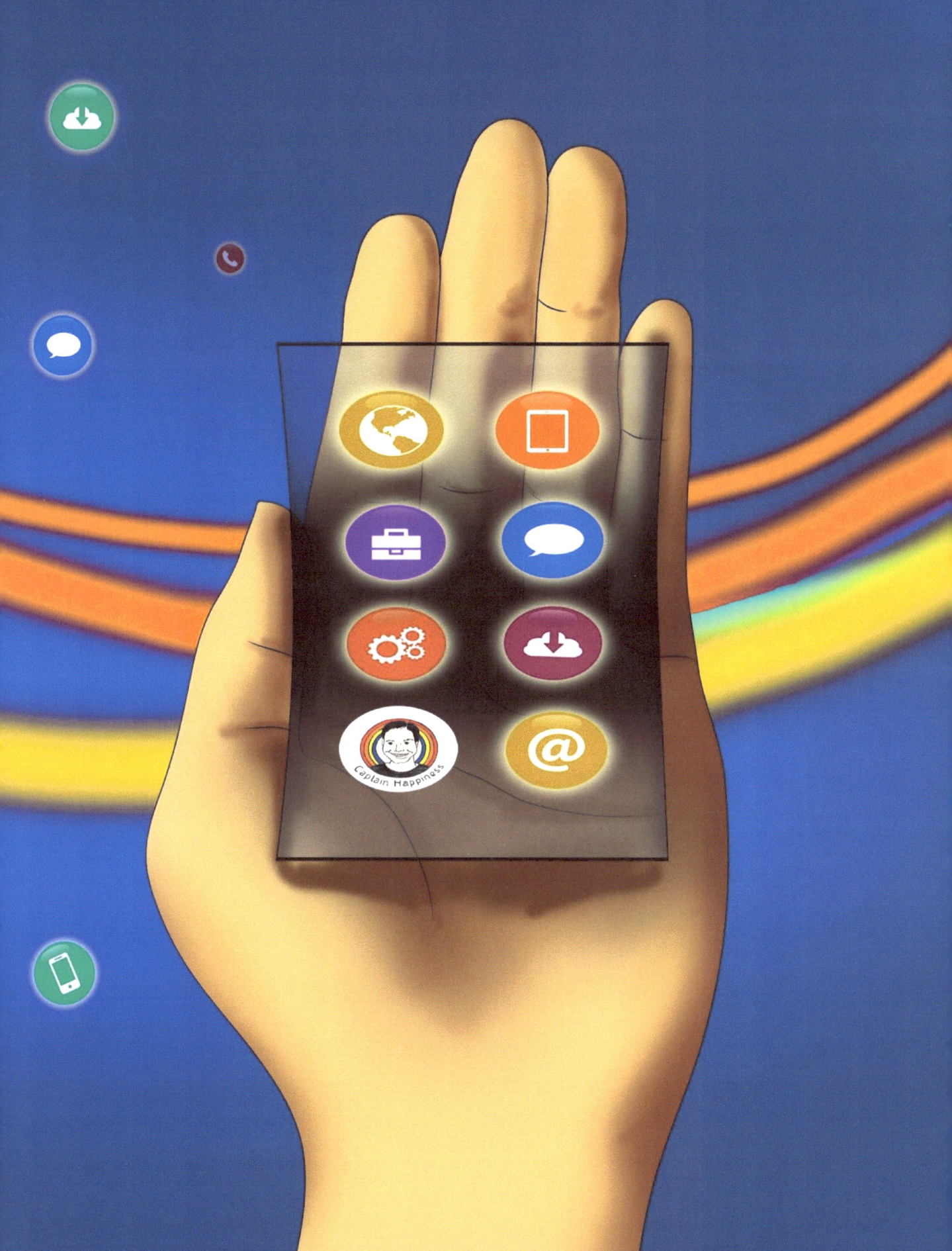

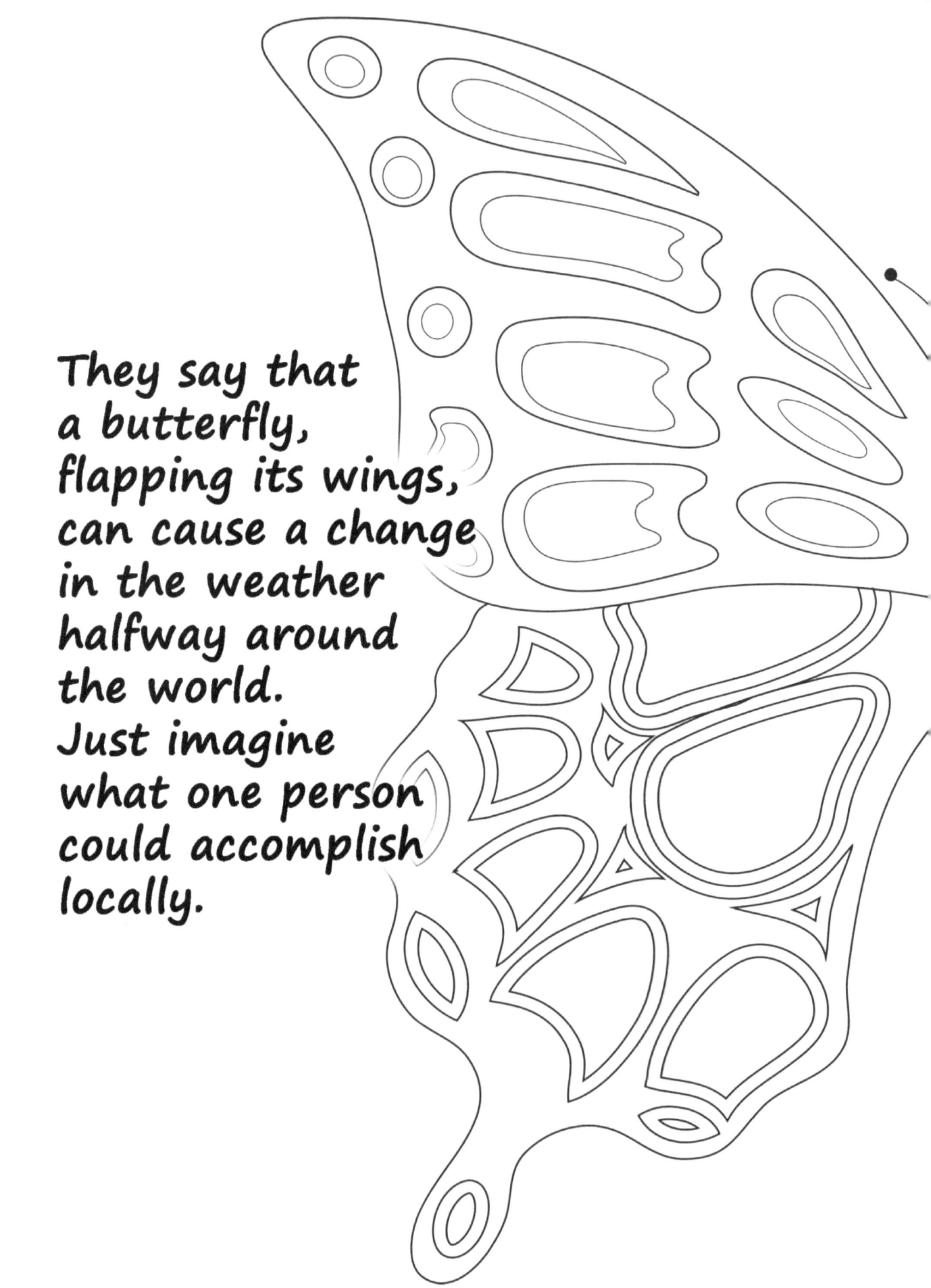

They say that a butterfly, flapping its wings, can cause a change in the weather halfway around the world. Just imagine what one person could accomplish locally.

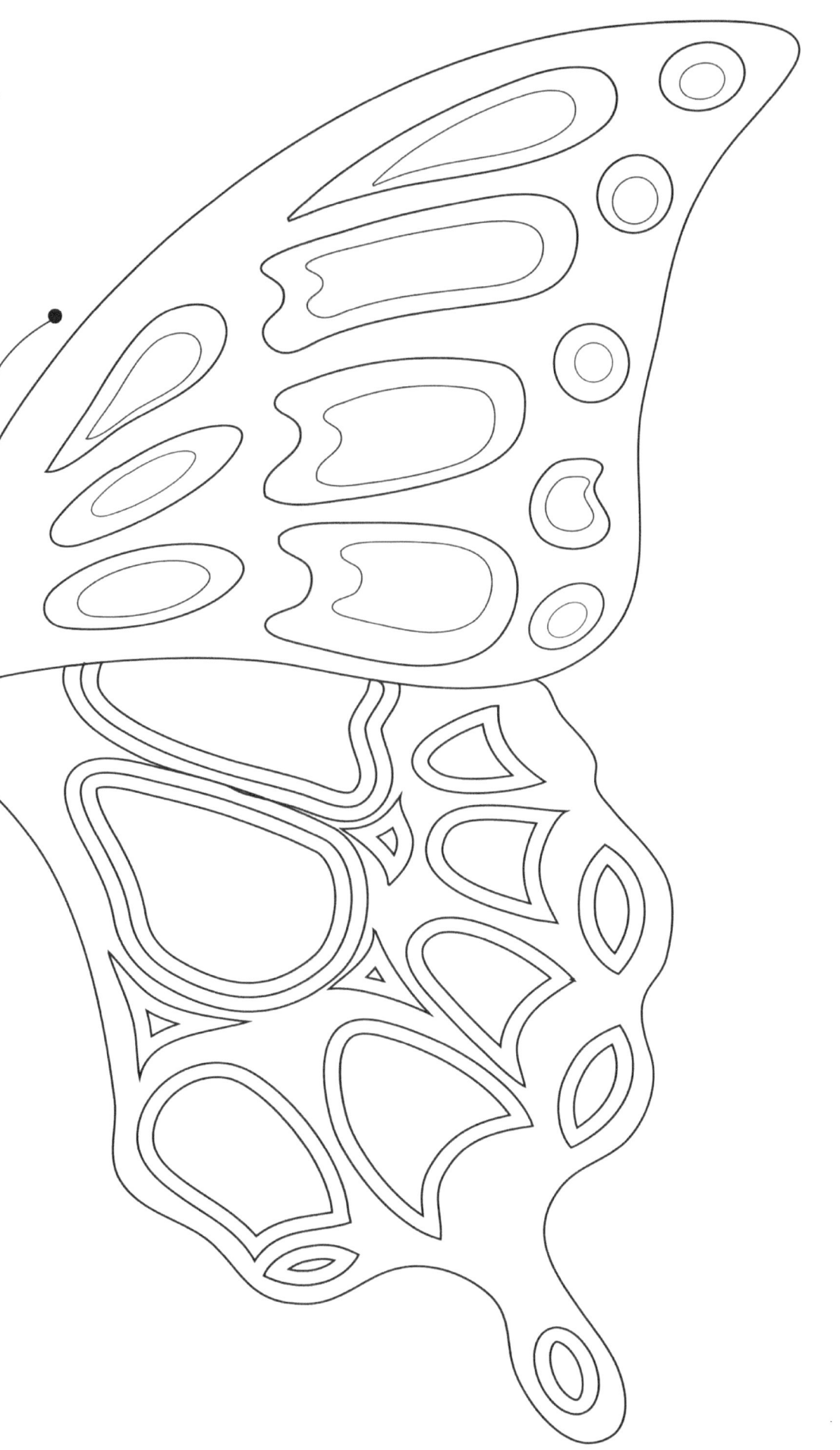

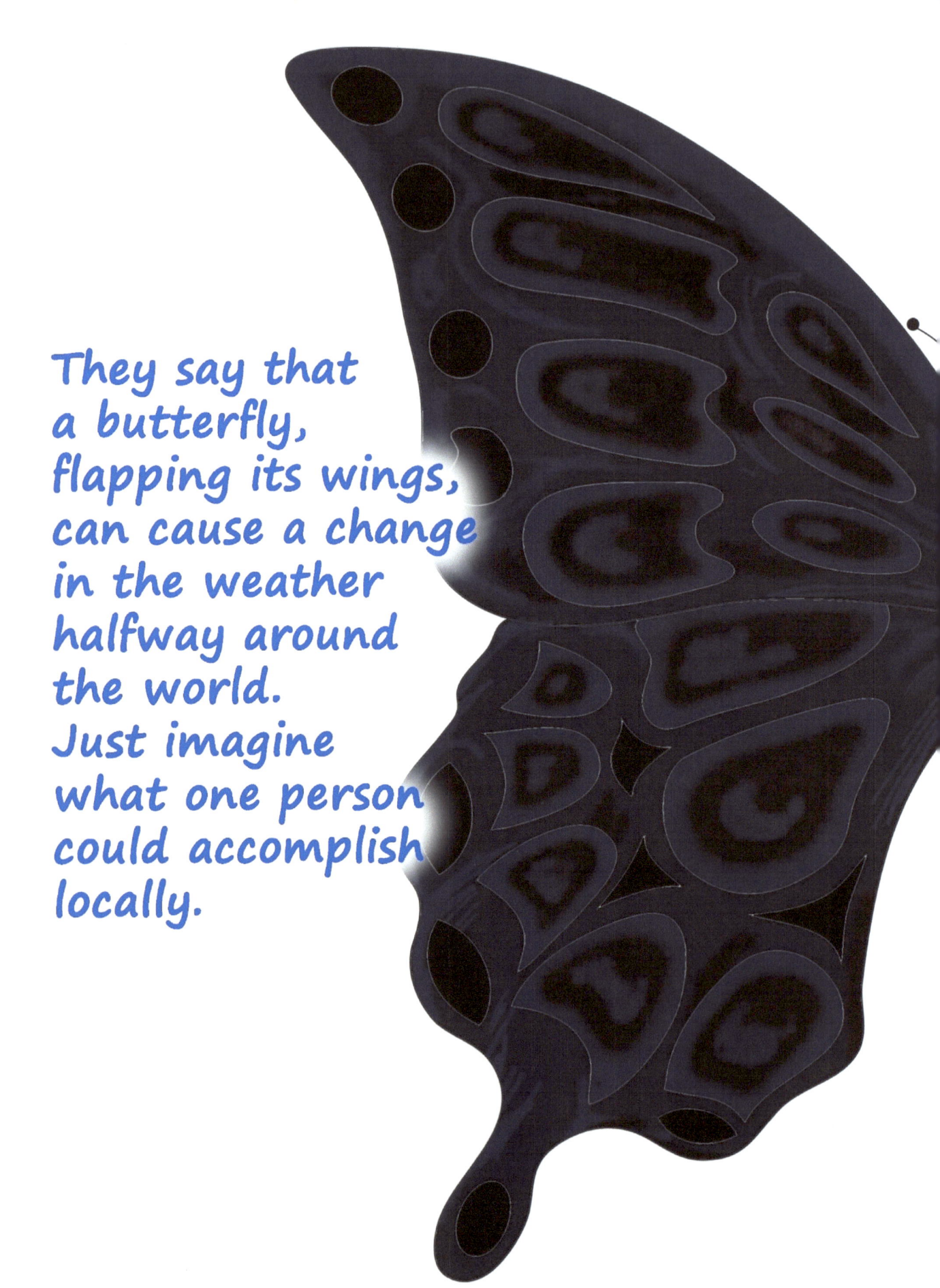

They say that a butterfly, flapping its wings, can cause a change in the weather halfway around the world. Just imagine what one person could accomplish locally.

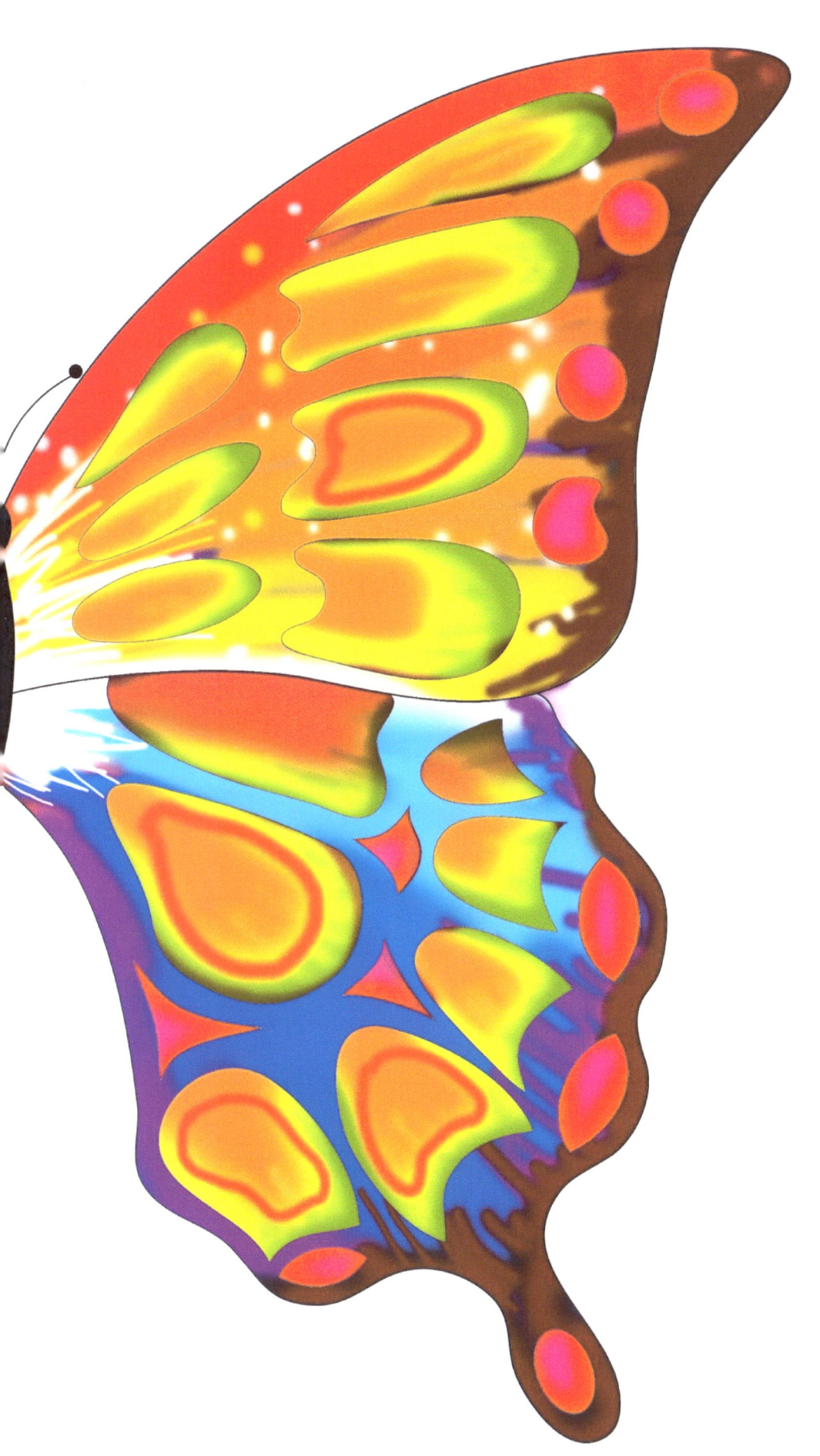

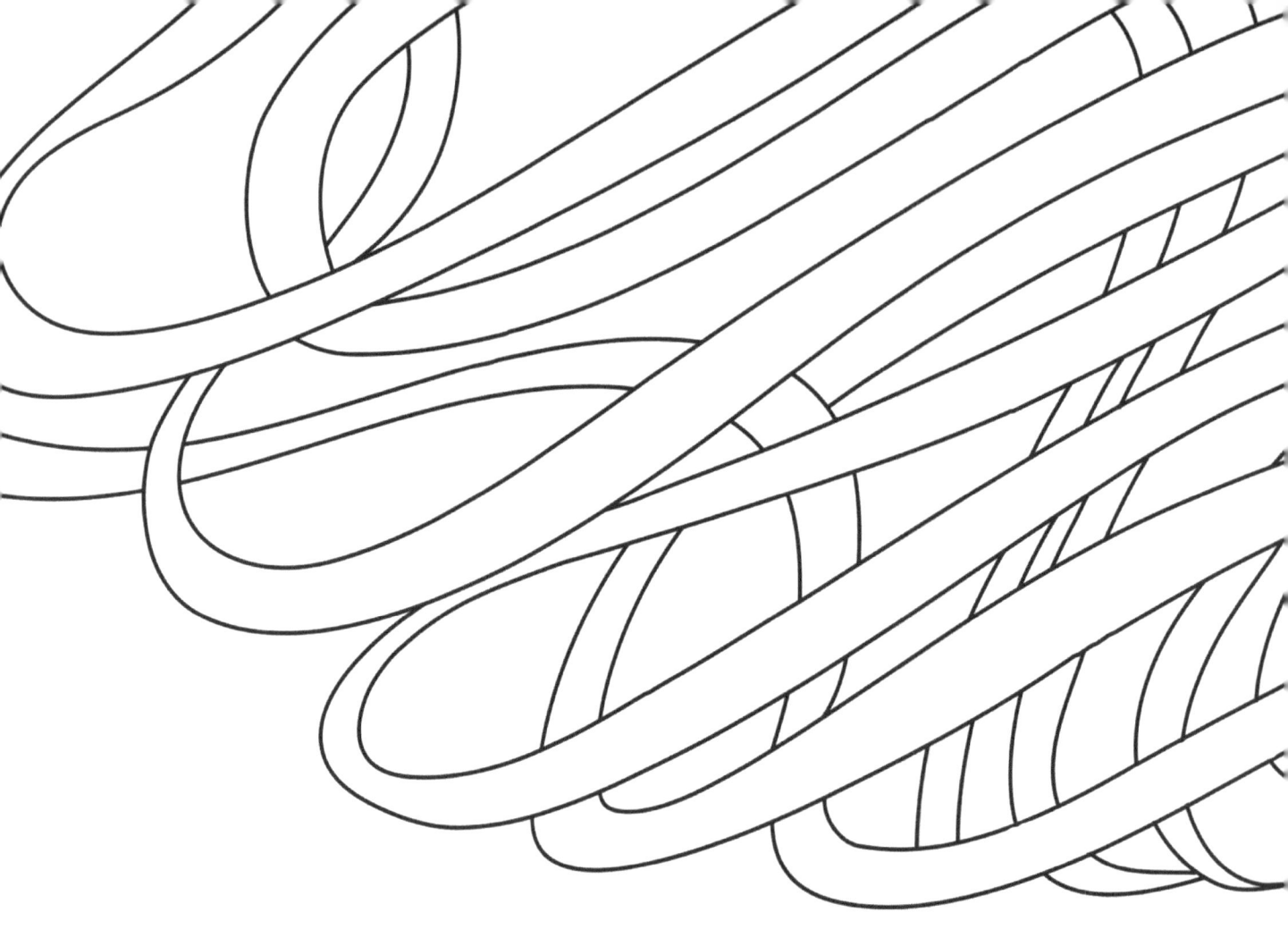

**Life can not be lived in reverse.
Knowledge thinks of the past while imagination is the future.
Just imagine what the future holds.**

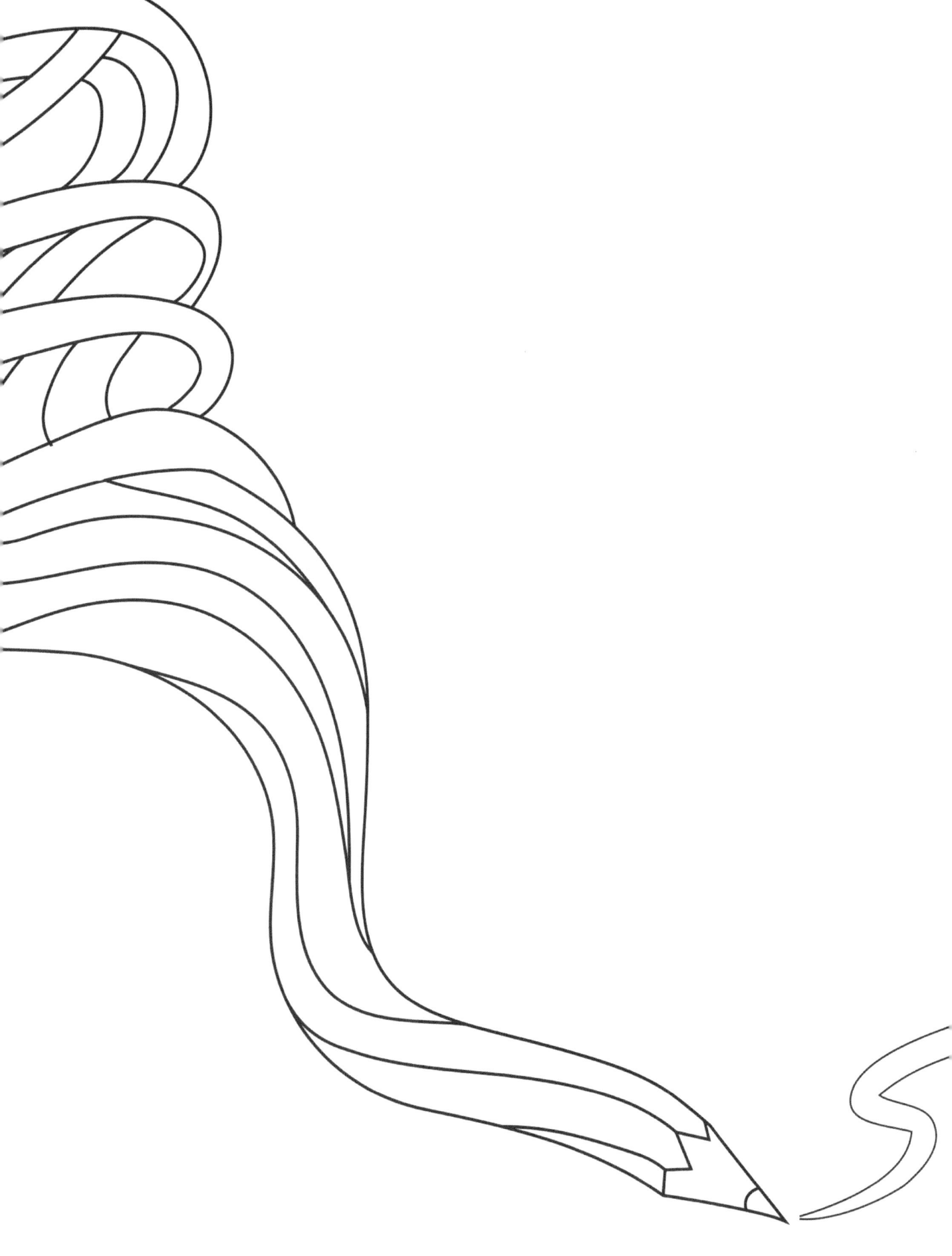

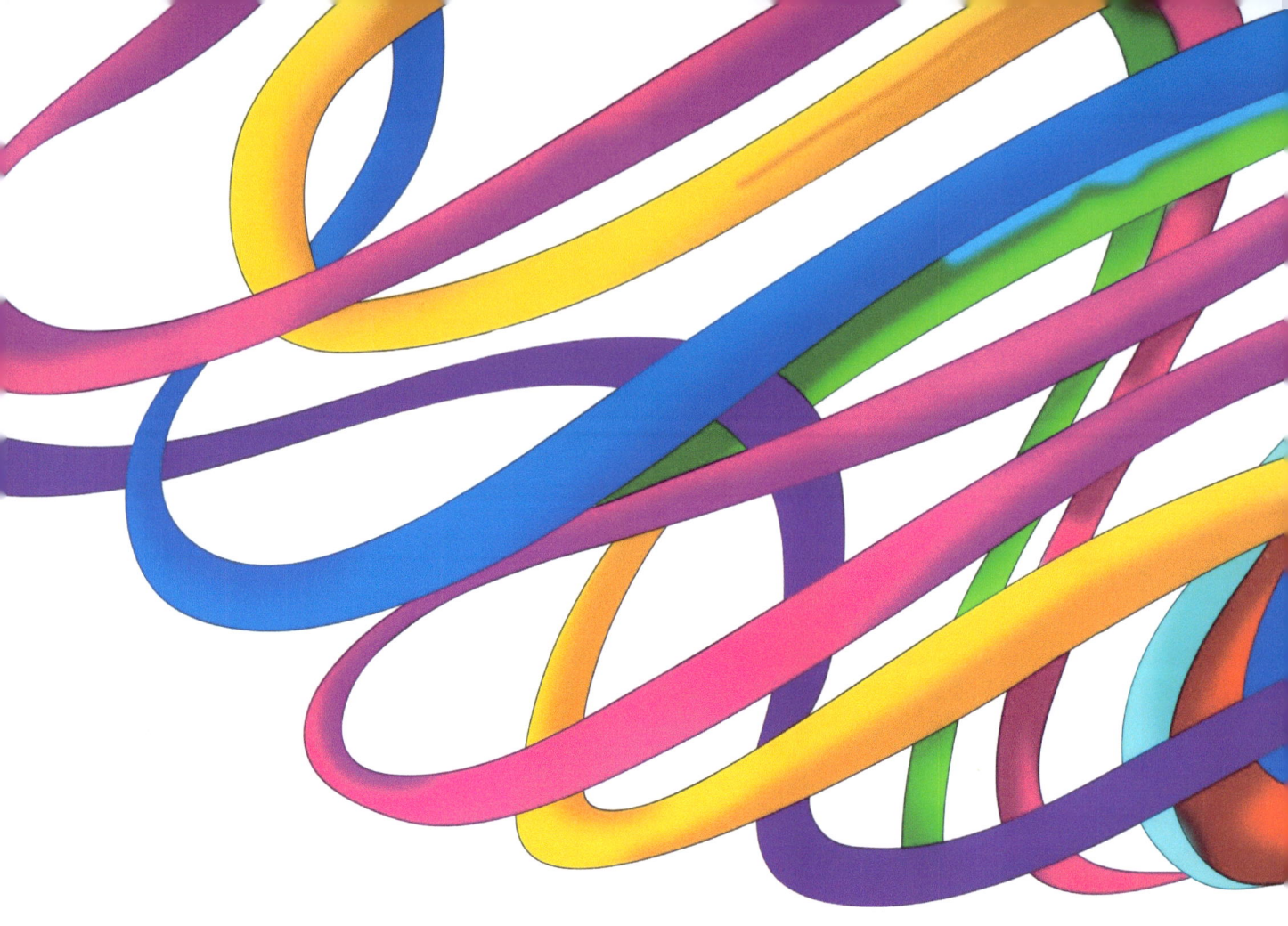

Life can not be lived in reverse.
Knowledge thinks of the past while imagination is the future.
Just imagine what the future holds.

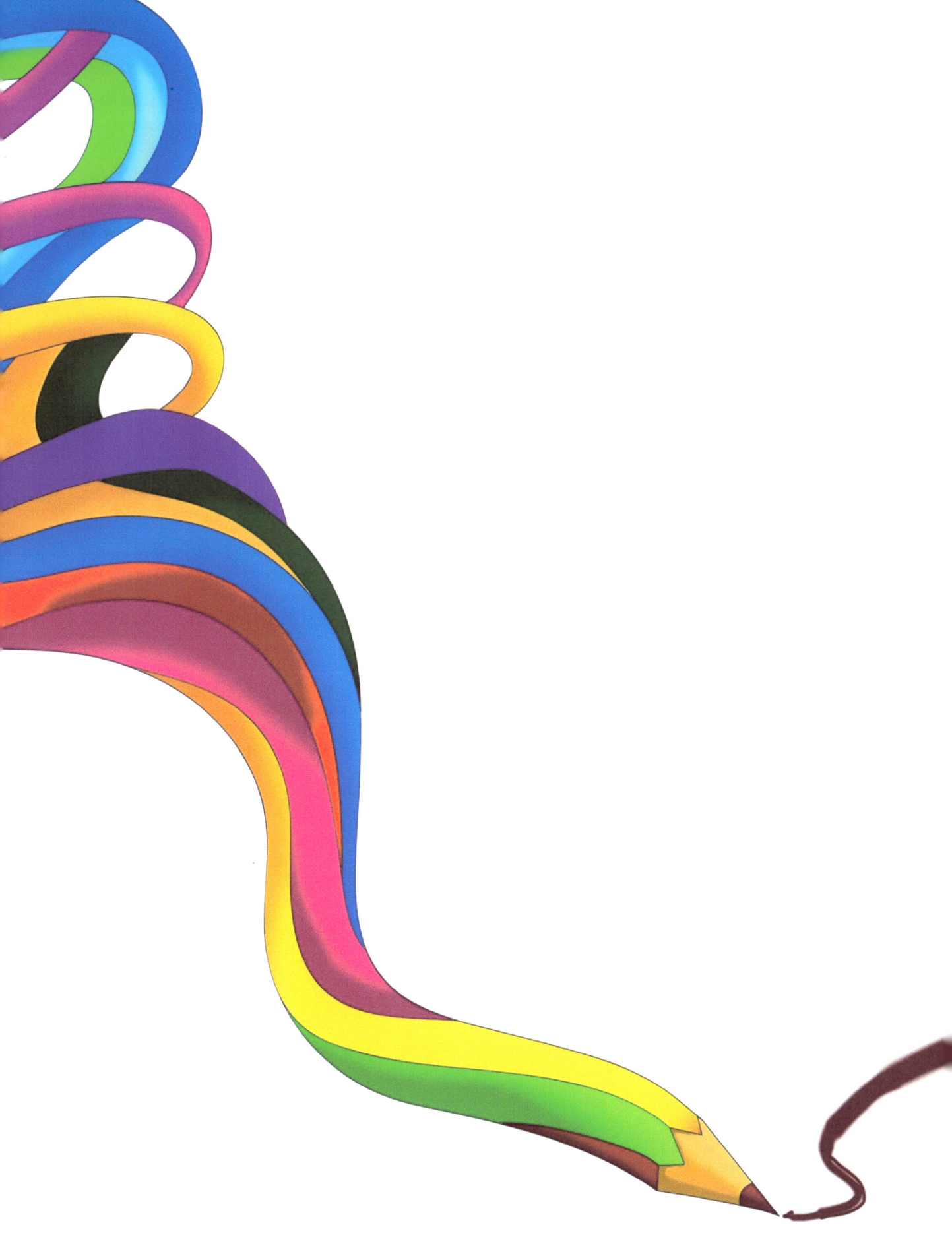